THE SASQUATCH PARADOX

LEVI MACHOVEC

CONTENTS

AUTHOR'S NOTE

After writing *A Quest for the Truth*, which at the time I believe represented the pinnacle of my capabilities, something dawned on me. One book would simply not be enough for me to fully expand on the ideas needed to further legitimize my argument. As proud as I was of my first book, I must admit that it was far from perfect. At the time, I was hindered by the challenges of self-publishing, the rushed nature of the book's release (due to relocating to an area three hours from home), as well as the ignorance that comes from writing and publishing a book for the first time. Rereading my original book left me with mixed emotions. As stated above, publishing the book was an achievement of which I was proud in and of itself. However, the competitive person within was left feeling somewhat deflated. I want to hold myself entirely accountable for my own mistakes and those in my first book. First, there were many grammatical errors in the book. As far as I am concerned, one grammatical error is too much. The editor that I had for the first book was nothing short of phenomenal, but I feel that I let him down by having a book with grammatical mistakes in it. I focused too much on getting the book published and released. I did not slow down enough to catch the mistakes I had made.

As for the title, there are some who disagree with my calling myself a historian. Here are my thoughts on this controversy. First, I believe that an undergraduate degree is sufficient for calling oneself a historian. However, I concede that there are some who believe that this title is earned through a graduate degree. Second, my belief was that I had earned the title by having written and published a book on a historical topic. Third, as a young man trying to make a name for himself in a field that lacks serious consideration from major academic and scientific institutions, I acknowledge that one can say that I stretched my title to make me appear more qualified than what some skeptics would consider me to be. So, if my use of this title offended you, or if you feel that I have not yet earned the label "historian," I would like to sincerely apologize. My intentions were not to claim to be something that I am not. My intent was only to open the eyes of the readers to the phenomenon that is Sasquatch.

Here is my promise to you. I promise that this book will in no way have been rushed and that I will hold the end product to the highest standard of that which I want to produce. Although some parts of the book cover the same material as *A Quest for the Truth*, I have reorganized these sections into a more cohesive and concise structure. Additionally, I expand on some of the ideas presented in the first book—mainly on the Patterson Gimlin Film. One last thing before we get to the book. To all of those who are reading this book, and to all of those who purchased my first, the fact that you are open-minded enough to read a book on this topic makes me truly grateful. You have my sincerest thanks, and I truly hope that you enjoy this book.

INTRODUCTION

The book you are holding right now shares many similarities with my first, *A Quest for the Truth*. While there are many similarities between the two, the differences far outnumber them. The subject remains the same, but the argument has changed. The first book's sole purpose was to argue for the existence of Sasquatch by show demonstrating that there is, in fact, sufficient evidence to warrant scientific investigation. While this book shares a similar theme, the main argument has changed.

We will still review the best evidence for the existence of Sasquatches. Much of the evidence used is the same as that in *A Quest for the Truth*. And yet, the ideas presented in that book must be expanded upon. After examining the evidence, this book will seek to explore and explain why the Sasquatch as a subject has yet to be taken seriously by the scientific community. Of course, there has always been natural resistance to any discovery made throughout history, especially after the formation of the scientific process. However, in terms of the subject of Sasquatches, something else entirely has happened. The natural resistance to an idea, any idea, was meant to cull the weak from the strong theories, thereby refining and bolstering the arguments in its favor. With the notion of

Sasquatches, academic skepticism has subtly morphed into artificial defiance that threatens to indefinitely postpone the (re)discovery of relict hominoids. The term *relict hominoids* refer to Sasquatch-like entities from around the globe that have managed to survive extinction.

The research from my first book laid the foundation for the research into this book. From my investigations, it was obvious that a strange phenomenon was occurring in the scientific community, one which I was (at the time) unable to name. After continued research and contemplation of the evidence, I could finally label this phenomenon: artificial defiance. The book gets its title from this defiance (which will be discussed in greater detail in the second half of the book). The explanation of artificial defiance would be of little consequence to you if you were unaware of the high-quality evidence that exists.

As you read *The Sasquatch Paradox: Scientific Defiance to the Recognition of Relict Hominoids*, keep this quote, which the Devil himself once told Napoleon Hill, firmly in mind, "Remember this: everything having a real existence is capable of proof."[1]

This is your last chance. After this, there is no turning back. You take the *blue* pill—the story ends, you wake up in your bed and believe whatever you want to believe. You take the *red* pill—you stay in Wonderland, and I show you how deep the rabbit hole goes. Remember: all I'm offering is the truth. Nothing more.[2]

1

THE PATTERSON-GIMLIN FILM

In 1982, Ridley Scott released one of the greatest movies of all time, the science fiction classic *Blade Runner*. If you have read my first book, you may have an inkling of where I am going with this section. Sitting on the roof of an abandoned building, Rick Deckard, played by Harrison Ford, is confronted by the psychotic replicant Roy Batty, played by Rutget Hauer. On that rooftop, Batty (Hauer) delivers one of the most iconic lines in movie history (quoted at the beginning of *A Quest for the Truth*). Deckard is trapped by the physically superior Batty, who is near death. As he corners Deckard, he approaches as if he were a tiger just about to take down its prey. However, something miraculous happens. Instead of killing Deckard, Batty delivers his famous monolog, which begins with the iconic words forever etched in the memory of movie fans: "I've seen things you people wouldn't believe." Anyone watching this scene would undoubtedly feel chills running down their spine. The evil replicant that was trying to kill anyone who stood in the way of its freedom had a chance to avenge his comrades. However, he chose to remain peaceful, showing Deckard—who was tasked with ridding the world of these defunct replicants—that they all wanted the same thing as him: to live.

So much can be written about the magnitude of the movie as a whole and that line specifically, but we must return our attention to Batty's iconic line, "I've seen things you people wouldn't believe." Its significance lies in the fact that it helps show us that what we thought of the replicants was simply and utterly false. However, the quote has a meaning outside of the movie that is applicable to a certain segment of the population. There exists a proportion of the population—much larger than one might assume—that claim to have seen something that "you people wouldn't believe." That something goes by many names, none more famous (or, perhaps, infamous) than Bigfoot.

There have been sightings of this creature for many years by many different people. People from different walks of life, across ages and cultures, have all reported encounters with these animals. Although there are over 10,000 reported encounters, there is one that is by far the most known, one whose sighting is arguably the most significant Bigfoot sighting in all of history. You might be asking yourself, what makes this man's encounter more significant than the rest? Well, the answer is quite simple, this man happened to have a film camera with him. And film this Bigfoot Roger Patterson certainly did, alongside his friend Bob Gimlin. (*Author's note: From this point forth, I will refer to Bigfoot as Sasquatch—or the plural, Sasquatches—due to personal preference for the term*).

While the reason for this sighting's fame is quite simple, everything else surrounding this film is not. Perhaps you are thinking that I left out one, all-too-familiar, detail: Sasquatches are not real. You might be saying to yourself that a film of a Sasquatch sighting is obviously no more than a hoax. Many people who doubt the existence of Sasquatches believe the answer is simple, the film has to be a hoax. Let me assure you of this: the Patterson-Gimlin Film (hereafter the PGF) is anything but simple.

Long before the PGF's filming, Roger Patterson rented a film camera (the same he would eventually use on that fateful October day). He rented the camera on May 13th, 1967.[1] Patterson, this average American, was about to become more than your typical American cowboy. Patterson had a unique belief: he was under the impression that there existed a large human-like primate living in the woods of North America. In fact, his belief was so firm that he released a book titled *Do Abominable Snowmen of America Really Exist?* (a book largely made up of newspaper stories of encounters with these animals). His interest can clearly be seen by his inclusion of a large number of artistic recreations of what he believed these animals looked like.

Come fall of 1967, Patterson and Gimlin traveled to Northern California to shoot some footage for Patterson's documentary. The location he chose was over 400 miles from his home in Yakima, Washington.[2] It may strike one as odd for him to have driven so far for his home, but there was a sighting not long before Patterson's arrival. Why would you not choose to visit a location with a recent sighting? The odds of finding, let alone filming, a Sasquatch are astronomically low, but, as the old adage goes, you miss 100% of the shots you do not take. You cannot film a Sasquatch unless you go out into the woods with a camera.

Patterson and Gimlin chose to travel the woods on horseback. On October 20th, they stumbled upon the very thing that Patterson so keenly sought. Although highly unlikely, it is well within the realms of possibility that Patterson was fortunate enough to position himself with a chance to film a Sasquatch: that is, if we assume that such an ape exists. After their supposed encounter, Patterson was left with a little over 23 feet of film.[3] If a picture is worth a thousand words, then the PGF is worth so much more. At the time of writing (during 2021), there has yet to be any exact consensus on the authenticity, or lack thereof, of this film. We will hopefully shed some light on this ever-continuing mystery. We will examine the most authoritative source on all things PGF, namely Bill Munns's book *When Roger Met Patty*. Munns's book may well be the definitive work on the entire subject as it provides an excellent argument on this mystery. Accordingly, it will be my primary source for the rest of this chapter.

Before we begin our analysis of the PGF, there are some elements of the film that I would first like to discuss. It was filmed on Friday, October 20th, 1967, in Bluff Creek, Northern California, at approximately 1:30 pm.[4] The film shows a hominid walking through a creek bed. The film either shows a man in a fursuit or an unidentified ape. The film lasts for approximately one minute and comprises 954 frames[5] shot with a Kodak K-100 film camera.[6] Skeptics and believers alike acknowledge all of these facts as being legitimate. If you have not seen the film, simply type "Patterson Gimlin Bigfoot Film" into YouTube. Once done, go to the filters and sort the results by view count. There will be a couple of different versions to view. Note, the video that shows all 100 feet of film roll is titled *"Patterson/Gimlin Bigfoot Film – Complete Version."* The complete footage also includes the B footage that Patterson shot before filming Patty. The other versions focus almost exclusively on the "lookback" sequence (where the Sasquatch seems to look at the camera). The figure was dubbed Patty, a female name, due to her breasts, and is also a play on the filmmaker's last name (Patterson). These are all facts that we will use as the foundation of the following argument.

Any filmmaker will tell you this; when creating a film, you want to make everything as simple as possible. There is so much that can, and will, go wrong when making a film. The last thing any filmmaker would do is to make life more difficult than it needs to be. The way filmmakers usually ease the process is by selecting the most convenient location, which can be passed off as another. Say you are a filmmaking company based in California and want to film a movie about living in Florida. Why film in Florida when you can pass off parts of California as Florida? The audience would be oblivious to this and the filmmaker saves a significant amount of money by remaining in California. Not only does this save money, but it avoids the considerable inconvenience of having to move all of your supplies and staff to and from the location.

This is something almost universally agreed upon by filmmakers and is by no means a point of contention. Bearing this in mind, let us consider the following question: why did Roger Patterson drive all the way to Northern California when he could have easily shot the "hoaxed" film in Washington? We can agree that any filmmaker would want to make the shooting process as easy as possible. It is, therefore, a fair inference to make that Patterson would want to make shooting his film as easy as possible also (if we assume that he hoaxed the PGF). As such, we can assume Patterson would have done the same. Patterson revealed owning a map detailing *"Where Hairy Giants Are Seen Most."* Five of the locations shown were near his Washington home, whereas only one was near the film site.[7]

As mentioned above, we know for certain that the film was shot in Northern California, as this has been independently verified by multiple different sources. If the film site's location was a point of contention, we would undoubtedly have heard more about it from skeptics. As skeptics have not advanced any arguments about the location, we can infer their agreement. The difficulties in filming far from your home stem from time, money, and transportation. Alone, each of these causes a problem. Combined, we would have to seriously question why Patterson would choose so challenging a film site. Of course, if the film was a happenstance due to both Patterson and Patty being at the same place at the same time, then the scenario would make much more sense. The only possible explanation would be that Patterson intentionally hoaxed the film far from home to lend greater weight to his deception. The natural counter to this argument would be that the last scenario is unlikely due to Patterson having never brought this up to anyone.

Knowing that the film site defies common sense, we can continue forward with our investigation to determine the PGF's authenticity. There is one more salient fact regarding the location that needs to be addressed. Roger Patterson lived in Yakima, Washington—that is beyond question. Another fact, albeit one that may seem inconsequential, is that most of Hollywood's special effects were done by people working within the industry. Indeed, it was notoriously difficult to break into Hollywood at this time. One would typically need a connection. This means that the best makeup artists of the time were those who knew someone in the industry and were able to learn the tricks and trades from the very best.[8] Needless to say, it was highly unlikely, at that time, for an outsider to begin working as a makeup artist. One of the few who did so was John Chambers. Chambers was the man who did the special effects for the 1968 science fiction classic *Planet of the Apes*. Chambers was not a Hollywood insider, nor did he know anyone who could have helped him get a job in Hollywood. However, what Chambers did have was a special talent. He created and built prosthetic devices for those injured in war. He became extremely proficient in his craft. Indeed, so much so that when he noticed that his techniques were superior to those used in Hollywood, he wrote NBC a letter. He detailed how he could apply his skills to help create more realistic makeup and special effects than what they were currently using.

What followed is now movie history. He applied his craft to the movies and profited from his endeavors. Chambers, however, was not the only makeup artist who made it into the notoriously difficult-to-reach position of Hollywood makeup artist. Much like Chambers, Rick Baker had a special skill set that earned him his position in Hollywood. Baker always dreamed about making it to the big screen and, from a young age, worked tirelessly to hone his artistic craft. Baker had a distinct advantage that helped him achieve his goal: he lived near Hollywood. Although this may seem trivial, it is of far greater importance than it appears. Living in this location allowed Baker to be within easy driving distance of the stores which stocked the necessary materials for his craft. Granted, Baker often found himself driving across all of California in search of his supplies, but he still was able to get everything he needed. Moreover, Baker had to teach himself how to apply makeup. He had to continue to practice until he was skillful enough to showcase his talents to those in Hollywood.[9]

Before we continue, we need to expand on the idea of Chambers and Baker in relation to Patterson. There is clear documentation of the effort that Chambers and Baker exerted into becoming experts in their field. This same type of documentation does not exist for Patterson. There is clear evidence that Chambers worked with prosthetics. There is also evidence for Baker doing so in the form of a high school newspaper dubbing Baker "Rick Baker monster maker."[10] There is no such evidence for Patterson. This leads us to question Patterson's intent. Assuming that he hoaxed the PGF and that he knew a secret technique to build an ape suit far more realistic than anything seen in Hollywood, then why did he do nothing with this extraordinary talent? When I say nothing, I mean that he literally died without revealing his secret. What was his end goal? What did he have in mind when he hoaxed the film? Two common answers to these questions are that he hoaxed the film so as to gain both money and attention. This seems fair enough; after all, people have done significantly worse things for both of these ends. However, his methods seem rather ineffectual. Assuming he wanted fame and wealth, he could have easily achieved both had he come clean. Everyone would have had a laugh. More importantly, however, the film would serve as a way to showcase his talents in order to work in Hollywood or to sell his technique. Considering that Chambers had a budget of $1 million for *Planet of the Apes*,[11] then it makes sense that Hollywood would have wanted this same technique for themselves as they could have saved a substantial amount of money in the future. Although movies today are dominated by CGI, this would have been unforeseeable in 1967, meaning that Hollywood studios would have assumed that special effects would remain the norm.

Skeptics could counter my argument here by arguing that Chambers' work on *Planet of the Apes* focused on facial prosthetics, whereas Patty's was a full-sized fursuit, meaning that they are not a fair comparison. Such an argument is partially correct. I would concede that Baker's Kong suit would serve as a better comparison. However, there were those in Hollywood—Janos Prohaska to be specific—who argued that it would be impossible for Patty to have been a man in a suit. Prohaska, who worked in Hollywood from 1939 to the time he commented on the PGF in 1971, was the perfect expert to comment on the film. Prohaska created multiple gorilla costumes during his time in Hollywood, meaning that we should not discount his expertise. Prohaska argued that it would have had to have been a man who had hair glued to their body for a minimum of 10 hours.[12] This length of time (from an expert, no less) is highly significant. Patty was estimated to have been filmed at approximately 1:30pm. While Prohaska says that it was more likely to have been a man with hair glued on them, we can eliminate this possibility due to his 10-hour preparation estimate. Assuming a minimum of 10 hours—which, in all fairness, we should increase considering that Patterson did not have Prohaska's expertise—this would put Patterson in the woods of Northern California in the dark early morning hours, laboriously gluing hair onto an actor. Unless evidence to the contrary arises, we must assume that Patterson was a novice in the field of special effects. That would mean that Patterson would have been performing especially difficult work in the dark, in the middle of the woods. There are too many holes in this scenario. Where is this person? They would surely have stood to make money from revealing the hoax and their complicity (as well as from the ape suit as well). It is inconceivable that someone without practice could have done what Patterson is rumored to have done precisely because he did not have the requisite knowledge. Add to that the fact that much of the makeup work would have to have been done at night, and we see the unlikelihood of the hoax scenario.

To return to Baker's Kong suit, it might seem like an excellent suit to compare to Patty—and in some regards, it certainly is—yet the material used for the Kong suit was unattainable for Patterson. Baker used bear pelts for his suit, which were both costly and difficult to obtain.[13] If they were costly and difficult to obtain for Hollywood, then they would have been exceptionally more expensive and difficult to acquire for Patterson, an industry outsider. There are four suits I would like to compare to Patty. The first two are 1960s Japanese King Kong suits. The third comes from the spectacular 1968 movie *2001: A Space Odyssey*. The fourth, and most important for us, is another of Baker's creations. TOHO, the Japanese movie studio, is known for making monster movies. The most famous of all movie monsters, Godzilla, is a TOHO production. The two movies that include King Kong in the TOHO Kaiju films are 1962's *King Kong vs. Godzilla* and 1967's *King Kong's Escape*. They may not be Hollywood movies, but we can learn much from the suits used as they were made by one of the world's finest suit-making companies. The technique used by Hollywood (and TOHO) for creating ape suits during this time involved assembling the suit over the actor. It was done in steps, with the headpiece being put on separate from the chest piece.[14] It was done in this manner for easy access to the actor's head. The suits became extremely hot—so much so that one would risk the actor's death if they were unable to remove the suit in time. This is why everyone living in a cold part of the world is told to cover their head in winter: because a significant amount of heat is lost from the head if left uncovered. The reverse can be said of a covered head —instead of losing, it would intensify the heat. That is why suits were connected by the headpiece to the chest piece. Doing so, as Bill Munns says, results in a seam that is extraordinarily difficult to hide and usually becomes exposed by minimal movement from the actor.[15]

Munns details why this seam that existed on the back of the neck on ape suits in 1967 is of the utmost importance to search for when analyzing the PGF.

> It is one seam that simply must exist on the figure (if the figure is a suited human), and it is located in an area that virtually guarantees it is on the film. And the sometimes argued poor quality of the image, which is occasionally stated as not sharp enough for us to resolve details on the figure anatomy, is in fact sufficiently sharp to show flaws in a neck seam if such flaws did exist in the filming of a human in a suit... The head turn ("lookback") and the subsequent footage from the back showing the neck after the turn is quite literally a "worst-case scenario" for trying to keep a neck seam from showing.[16]

Munns continues this with:

> In 1967, the back of the beck on a fur costume was a pain... There was no great solution for the problems it caused, except to ask whoever is directing and staging

the mime to not show the back of the costume and back of the neck... If we had to show the back of the neck, the best plan would be for the mime to stand still, the makeup artist brushed out the fur to be as smooth as possible, and then film without letting the performer move around and especially not turn the head.[17]

Assuming Patterson hoaxed the PGF, having the actor in the suit turn their head was a monumentally incompetent decision as no technology then existed which could have allowed this movement while simultaneously disguising the seam.

The reason we compare the suits is simple: one of the best suit-making companies in the world could not come even close to creating anything resembling the realism of Patty. Had they had the ability to create a better suit, they would have done so. Indeed, a more realistic monster would have translated into larger audience numbers and, therefore, higher profits or accolades. Look no further than when Godzilla fights King Kong. Kong's movements are clearly those of a man in a suit. This is evidenced by the folds in the suit when Kong walks, as well as by the clear visibility of the seam that Munns describes. The 1967 version, which, admittedly, was low budget, was created by TOHO. It is a reasonable inference to make that the special effects team on that movie would have had more money and experience than Patterson. We can also assume that, further to their experience and money, they also would have had supplies from other movies. All of this helped them create the best ape suit that they could have done, which, it must be said, was far from realistic. These two suits are important because they show what talented people from outside of Hollywood could create.

Now, we will turn to our third ape suit, which came from the UK. For those who have not seen it, *2001: A Space Odyssey* is a science fiction masterpiece. As much as I would love to discuss both the movie and its implications for the science fiction genre, this would not help us solve the mystery of the PGF. However, the movie can help us in the form of the ape suits seen in its opening sequence.

These ape suits were created by Stuart Freeborn, who was tasked with creating the suits by none other than Stanley Kubrick. Of all the notoriously difficult stars to work with in the movie-making business, Kubrick was arguably the most challenging. Kubrick has a reputation as being one of the best directors in history, but this magnificent talent came at a price. He would often torment cast and crew members to ensure that he received the best performances and so that his vision could come to light. Look no further than the set of *The Shining*, where he bullied Shelley Duvall (to the point of her suffering from severe emotional distress) or demanded over 140 takes of one scene.[18] Knowing this, we can safely assume that Freeborn's work must have been of the highest possible standard. The suits that Freeborn made were marvelous. They created a sense of realism in the scene that is also found throughout the entire movie. However, when comparing the suits to Patty, they are nowhere near up to her quality. Freeborn and Kubrick were aware of the limitations that existed with their material and technology, so they applied a clever trick to their suits: they covered them with long hair so as to hide any visible faults. This technique was implemented perfectly in the movie. This is where the comparison becomes so important. Comparing Patty to the apes from *2001*, we can see that Patty is clearly far more realistic. It is highly significant that, compared with Freeborn's apes, Patty is short-haired. Why would one of the best directors in history demand long hair? Simple, to hide the flaws within his suits. Why did Roger choose not to use long hair when "creating" Patty? The simple thing to have done would have been to use long hair to hide any faults from the camera, but that is clearly not what we see in the PGF. How did Patterson create a better suit than Stuart Freeborn?

A further difference between the PGF and *2001* is that, in the former, we can see the back of the subject's neck (whether real or an ape suit). More specifically, we can see the clear movement of the head. Let us reconsider what Munns said: for it to be an ape suit, there must have been a seam connecting the head and neckpieces. To expand on this, we can further consider Munns's thoughts on the head turn. He regarded it as a worst-case scenario. As he did not want to expose the seam, Kubrick did not show any of his apes undertaking such a movement. The seam had to exist in an ape costume. There is no other way around it. Are we really going to assume that Patterson created a suit using a technique better than anything available to the industry? Freeborn used long hair to hide the mistakes in *2001*. He knew he needed the long hair after seeing the imperfections that existed on those suits. Had Patterson created a suit, why would he not do the same? One of the best special effects professionals in the world used long hair to cover the visible seam, so why did Patterson choose not to do so? One answer would be to return to the inference that he used a (self-developed) master technique to create Patty. However, this scenario presents more questions than it answers. The same question remains as to why he did not sell this technique. Moreover, how did a man with no experience in making ape suits (the lack of evidence means we can infer this unless proven otherwise) come to acquire a master technique? Knowing of the limited technology that existed in 1967, how Patterson pulled off this hoax is quite perplexing indeed.

The last suit we will discuss is another of Baker's creations, except this one has much more relevance to the topic as the suit in question comes from the movie *Harry and the Hendersons*. Said movie is about a family that has a Sasquatch live with them for a short period of time after they hit it with their car. The movie was made in 1987, 20 years after the PGF. There are two things to keep in mind with this analysis because there are two outcomes: either the suit is similar to Patty, which makes it plausible that Patty was an actor in a suit, or it is not of the same standard as Patty, which would lead us to believe that Patty was a biologically real animal. We know that if Baker created a suit of the same standard 20 years after, then it would be in the realm of possibility that Patterson could have created a suit (albeit two decades earlier). However, we would have to also discuss the technological and material advances in order to fully test and accept such a theory. We can safely assume that if Baker; with over 10 years experience, with advanced materials and technology, and all of the tools he could need at his disposal thanks to Hollywood and its vast resources, and with the perfection of his craft over time could not have created a suit similar in quality and realism to Patty, then we would have to infer that Patty was, in fact, a biologically real animal. We can make this inference as there are only two options: either Patty is a man in a suit or an unidentified ape. Eliminating one option would considerably strengthen the other. In sum, if a master craftsman with the best technology, materials, and an enormous budget cannot create something, it would be impossible for someone to do so without these four things (experience, technology, materials, and Hollywood's vast resources).

There are clear and noticeable differences between Patty and Harry. First, Harry appears to be much larger than Patty, which does not necessarily mean that we should assume Harry to be heavier. Second, Patty's head is much smaller. Third, Patty has a larger brow ridge than Harry. To the first point, so far, the evidence above has pointed to Patty being a real animal. Knowing that Harry is not real, we can assume that, although he appears taller, he would not have been heavier. This is not absolute, but we can reasonably infer that Patty–being biologically real—would weigh more due to the fact that it would entail having more developed muscles and an overall larger quantity of water in the body. Patty also has fat deposits, which, combined with her muscles, would add considerable weight to her frame. The water weight, fat, muscles, and skin/hair on Patty would result in a heavier weight than a man in a suit. The suit would undoubtedly be heavy, but it would unlikely be significantly so as the actor would then not be able to move. This does absolutely nothing to determine Patty's authenticity, but it is still important to examine every possible detail. Furthermore, this helps show how Patty left such deep imprints in the sandy creek banks on that distant October day.

As for the second and third differences listed above, those go much further than size differences in solving this mystery. The head shape and brow ridge are both highly significant, and we will discuss them in tandem. To better understand the differences, you will have to fully understand the anatomy of an ape's head. Humans and apes, although they share many similarities, have different skull compositions. As such, they have differently shaped skulls, which must be accounted for by those in the special effects industry when creating an ape suit. Humans have much larger brains than great apes. Our skulls must be shaped in such a way that allows for growth and provides protection.

> Apes have a head that goes back once the brow ridge is formed above the eye socket. The human head, by comparison, goes up into the cranial vault instead of back.[19]

This quote, based on Munns's experience in the movie industry, helps explain the differences in shape. Munns knew that, due to these differences, an anatomically correct ape suit would be impossible to create if you wanted to place an actor within it. He further explained:

> To make a gorilla mask, cheat the forehead higher than it actually is, to accommodate the human head inside, but make it look small by enlarging other aspects of the head.

The pictures contained in the picture index at the back of the book exemplify Munns's description of the skull. You will see what Munns was detailing when he talked about the formation of the brow ridge and the projection back to the point of the skull. With Harry's suit, we can note the absence of a brow ridge. Instead, we see that Baker used Munns's above method. This is clear and definitive proof that Patty has a skull that is anatomically similar to other great apes. In comparison, we have Harry, who shows clear signs of being fake. Of course, he does; he was meant to be. However, we know that, based on our above assumptions, we must accept Patty as real. Baker earned his living by creating realistic ape suits. Had he refined his abilities, he could have created more realistic suits, which would likely have resulted in more money for both the studio and himself. Even if Baker had not received more money from this movie by designing a superior suit, he could easily have signed future contracts guaranteeing him more (better paid) work. Baker did not create an ape suit more realistic than Patty. Why? Simply because he could not do so. It just was not possible in 1987. We can properly infer that if Baker could not have created a suit anywhere near the caliber of Patty, then neither could (the significantly under-experienced) Roger Patterson.

While you may think there is, as yet, insufficient evidence to accept Patty as real, we will further expand on information from that day to strengthen our argument. There is much more that we need to dive into. As mentioned above, Patterson rented the camera he used on May 13th, 1967. This becomes a point of interest when we consider that the rental period was for two days. This is where the story becomes convoluted. Skeptics use this as an opportunity to destroy Patterson's reputation. They do so because Patterson did not return the rental camera until long after the rental period had expired. Due to this, there was a warrant out for Patterson's arrest.[20] However, we must understand that attacking Patterson's character does absolutely nothing to destroy the validity of the PGF. One could (very unreasonably) make the claim that not returning the camera made him a bad person. What one cannot claim is that this warrant meant that he had bad intentions with regard to the PGF. Simply put, this is an unsound argument often advanced by skeptics, which is nothing more than an ad hominem attack on Patterson's character.

Examining the camera rental further actually strengthens the authenticity claims. Why would Patterson rent the camera in May but keep it until October? Frankly, if he was planning on hoaxing the PGF, then this was a highly stupid thing to do. We can infer that if Patterson did "hoax" something of this magnitude, then he had to have been fairly intelligent to do so. This is by no means a stretch; it just logically follows from those who claim it was a hoax. There is a big contradiction that occurs here. Why would a smart man risk jeopardize the hoax? Renting the camera closer to the film date would have been much smarter. Renting the camera in May and not returning it would have (and, eventually, did) cause more trouble for Patterson. There was a warrant out for his arrest. Imagine that the police had gone to Patterson's home to arrest him. They would have searched the premises to find the camera. Not only would they have found it, but they also would have found evidence of Patterson honing his craft. The jig would have been up, the hoax over before it began. Hoaxing such an event is not illegal. However, the cat would have been out of the bag. While the police could not have prevented Patterson from staging the hoax, they would have been able to provide damning evidence of the event's fabrication. Of course, this is all hypothetical because Patterson did not hone his craft but rather filmed a biologically real animal that October day.

Still need convincing? If so, congratulations on your skepticism, although a warning is due. Skepticism is useful, but too much of it can be a bad thing. At some point, you might become so close-minded that you prevent yourself from being convinced of anything. Remember, Socrates, one of the greatest thinkers in all of human history, was (and is) revered as a great philosopher not because he was close-minded but because he was more open to new ideas than all of his contemporaries.[21] That said, if you are still skeptical due to your belief that I have not yet made a strong enough argument, then I will continue to try and convince you.

Another thing that we ought to discuss is how the scientific community reacted to the PGF. Scientists then, and still today, were not impressed with the film. They dismissed it as no more than a hoax. At that time, the scientific community believed that the film was fake due to the way that Patty walked.[22] They argued that due to Patty being female (evidenced by her having breasts), she should have walked like a human female. As we said above, humans have large brains. Human babies are also born with large skulls—much larger than apes. Accordingly, females need wider hips to fit the human head through the birthing canal, which is why women walk differently from men.[23] We do not have to accept the scientific community's criticism due to their having made a major faulty assumption in their argument: they assume that a bipedal ape would share the exact same walking characteristics as humans, based only on the fact they both walk on two legs. Apes, however, are not born with large heads, meaning that female apes do not need wider hips to fit the baby's head through the birthing canal. Therefore, the argument made against the PGF by those scientists in 1967 and after were wrong.

Scientists have tended to make another large error regarding their analysis of the film. Except, this time, the mistake lies in what they did *not* say. Scientists assumed that they were the right people to solve the PGF mystery. They failed to contact the experts. Scientists are experts in most fields, but not when it comes to making ape suits—Hollywood insiders must be awarded that title. Luckily enough, two Hollywood experts did comment on the PGF: John Chambers and Janos Prohaska. Both men were considered to be at the top of their respective fields. They both created ape suits/ape special effects during their time in Hollywood, meaning that they were excellently qualified to provide reliable and informed opinions on the subject. Chambers has a unique claim to his name. For many years he was believed to have been the man who created the Patty suit. In fact, these rumors reached him, but he did comment upon them. That is until he was much older. 30 years after the PGF, Chambers admitted the truth: he had had no involvement whatsoever with the film. Chambers took this even further. While he accepted that he was very skilled with his craft, the suit was beyond anything that he could have created. Chambers even went on to argue that Patty must have been a biologically real animal.[24] If you think that Chambers was lying, know that he would have been far too busy working on *Planet of the Apes* to have had time to create the Patty suit. As for Prohaska, we have already briefly touched upon how he argued that the figure could not have been a man in a suit and that the only possibility was if it were a person with hair glued onto them. We know that this was highly improbable, to the point of being impossible, due to our discussion of the timeline. However, Prohaska did mention that the figure looked highly realistic and that a suit of that caliber was beyond his capability.[25]

If your mechanic tells you that you need to change your oil, you listen. If your doctor tells you that you need to lower your blood pressure, you listen. If your dentist tells you that you need to brush your teeth, you listen. If two of the best special effects artists in the history of Hollywood tell you that making a suit of Patty's caliber was beyond their abilities, you listen. It is because of this that we should begin to question scientists (whether then and now) about whether they have legitimate reasons for dismissing the existence of Sasquatches. "Are we sure the statement [scientists make in regard to Sasquatch] is based on firsthand knowledge, not personal interest or prejudice?"[26] Dave Ramsey says that if you want to become rich, listen to rich people. If you want to know if Patty could have been a man in an ape suit, listen to Hollywood professionals who make ape suits for a living.

We must also mention that there are certain anatomical details that are visible on Patty that could not have been replicated due to a lack of viable materials for their creation. There are many anatomical details that are worth examining, but we shall focus on three specifically: the breasts, triceps, and muscle herniation. We have to ask, why would Patterson have added breasts to the Patty suit? As in, why would Patterson have increased his workload? This point is an empirical fact. Scientists at the time, and researchers today, noticed the breasts. Making a female ape suit would have been considerably harder due to Patterson having to include breasts for realism. Patterson, if he had made a male suit, would not have needed to make genitalia because he could have hidden them while filming, as long as the groin of the suit was facing away from the camera. So why did he add the breasts? There were no materials at the time used in Hollywood that could have created the fluidity that we see in Patty's breasts. During the look-back sequence, we can see Patty extend her right arm. When she does this, we can see her triceps flex. To view this in greater detail, please visit the Bigfoot Field Researchers Organization (BFRO) expedition page to see a GIF that shows both the flexing of the triceps and the breasts. Spandex was not used at this time in Hollywood.[27] As such, the material available did not have this type of flexibility. Bear pelts were also used, but we can infer that Patterson did not use this due to their high cost and difficulty to acquire. Fur cloth was not flexible and would not have been able to show the triceps flex. In fact, nothing in Hollywood could have done this. Lastly, there is the visible muscle herniation. When walking, Patty turns to look at Patterson (the "look-back"). As she does this, it appears as if she takes a misstep. We see a ripple go up her leg. The ripple occurs in the same location as what we would expect from a muscle herniation of the quad. "When present in the thigh usually occur over the quadriceps, specifically over the vastus lateralis muscle... the bulge apparent on the thigh of Patty is prominent precisely at the period of the step cycle when the vastus lateralis is contracting and abates when the muscle is relaxed."[28] These three constitute three different aspects of Patty that would have been beyond the capability of Patterson—or, indeed, anyone—to have made.

Bill Munns referred to the look-back sequence as the worst-case scenario, as any movement of the head would risk exposing the seam that connects the head and chest pieces. It should be mentioned that skeptics could potentially argue that the head and chest pieces could have been combined into one piece, thereby allowing Patterson to film Patty in a manner that any other filmmaker would have avoided. However, there is a reason that people working in special effects did not use the single-piece technique: it was considerably dangerous for the actor. Suits become tremendously hot and working in one, even for a short amount of time, will rapidly raise the suit's temperature. Think back to a time when you wore sweaty clothes on a hot summer's day. You try to take them off, but the clothes stick to your body. This same thing would happen, only in a more extreme way because your entire body would be covered by a suit. Due to the suit, you would begin to sweat profusely, meaning that the suit would be impossible to remove. As Munns has said, yes, it is possible that Patterson did that very thing and built an upper body piece with a connected chest and headpiece. However, due to the risks involved for the actor, it would be highly implausible.[29]

The look-back sequence is of the utmost significance as it offers the clearest, closest look at Patty. Once again, this defies conventional wisdom. Why would Patterson have his actor move in such a way as can be described as the worst-case scenario? Moreover, why would Patterson do this when he is the closest to the subject? Patterson could have easily shown the look-back from further away, thereby minimizing his (still high) risk. Instead, he chose to be close during this worst-case scenario movement. Had Patterson happened upon Patty by chance (she, being a real animal), then all of these scenarios we discuss make perfect sense. They do not when we think of Patty as being an actor in a suit. Think back to school when someone you knew (not you, of course) would cheat on their work. They knew to take measures to disguise their cheating from the teacher. By doing this, the cheaters minimize their risk. Patterson did the opposite: he maximized it. Showing the look-back when he was closest to Patty is another example of how the film defies logic—that is, if you believe it to be a hoax. When considering the film as not having been faked, the film fits perfectly into our understanding of Patty's status of being a real animal.

Patterson had a film camera, which required a film reel. Patterson was filming Patty at the end of his reel. This means that, had he made a mistake during the "hoax," he would have had to load a new film into the camera. This would have taken time and the actor would have been at an increased risk of overheating and dehydration while waiting for Patterson. If Patterson had made a mistake, he would have had to start from the beginning. Put yourself in his shoes. If you planned on faking this film, would it not make much more sense to have a new reel in the camera so as to maximize shooting time. Made a mistake? No problem. Simply slice off the bad reels and move on. From Munns's analysis, we know that the original film shows no signs of slicing, meaning that Patterson loaded that camera with a reel, used it up, and changed it once he ran out. He did not doctor the film in any way after filming Patty.[30]

It is common scientific practice, when there are two theories, that the one chosen to explain an event is the theory that makes the least amount of assumptions. Which theory makes more assumptions? That of the skeptics, which assumes the following: Patterson had the ability, and supplies, to make a physical ape suit better than any Hollywood has ever produced; Patterson was a willing and able con artist who took the secret of his hoax to his grave; Patterson destroyed or successfully hid the suit to hide the evidence, and the actor in the hoax has remained silent to this day. Another assumption that should be mentioned is that if the PGF is a hoax, then it is likely Patterson had practiced before staging this particular hoax. If so, where is this film? Think I am wrong? I know that most of you have at some point taken a photograph, but rarely have you looked at a picture the first time and said that it was good enough. The same would hold true for this "hoax." It is a reasonable inference to make that if Patterson hoaxed this, then he practiced because that would be the only way that he could have fooled everyone. Beginners' luck cannot possibly apply here. It would be improbably to the point of impossible to best an expert on one's first try. These are all either questions or assumptions that must be answered in order for us to favor the notion that Patterson hoaxed the PGF. The theory that Patterson filmed a real Sasquatch assumes the following: Sasquatches are real, and Patterson happened upon one due to favorable wind conditions that prevented the animal in question from smelling Patterson and Gimlin as they approached. Which one of these hypotheses makes fewer assumptions?

Skeptics claim that Patterson hoaxed the PGF (when I refer to skeptics, I mean to refer to those whose close-mindedness leads them to make poor arguments against the existence of Sasquatches: either among laypersons or scientists). They are, of course, perfectly able to make such a claim. However, the burden of proof now rests on their shoulders. "He obviously hoaxed it," a common calling card of skeptics, must now be proven. Make that claim, but now it is on you to validate it. Should you believe it obvious that the film was hoaxed, then surely so is the evidence. I would then reasonably demand to be shown the evidence that Patterson practiced suit making. Show me the evidence that he could have acquired the supplies necessary to create the suit. Show me the evidence that he had the ability both to include an anatomically correct breast and a muscle herniation in the leg long before the technology existed to do so. When I claim that the PGF was real, the burden of proof is on me to validate my argument, which I have just done with this chapter. However, the same holds true for those who claim it to be a hoax.

Before we move on, we must tie up a handful of loose ends. There is a man who has made his way around the internet claiming to have sold Patterson the suit he supposably used to hoax the PGF. Phillip Morris, whose videos can be found on the YouTube channel *therealcrazyfish*, is the man who claims to have sold Patterson the suit. This man tells of how Patterson created the ape suit. He sold the suit to Patterson, upon which Patterson made certain adjustments to finish the Patty suit. If making such a realistic-looking suit was as easy as this man claims, then why did Hollywood spend so much money on their ape suits when they could have saved millions by contracting this man's services? Moreover, where is the receipt showing that Patterson bought this suit? Where is the check used to buy the suit? We would require more than mere anecdotal evidence if we are to believe these claims. Chambers, Prohaska, and Baker were unable to create anything closely resembling the level of Patty. These men were true experts and pioneers in their field. They all possessed immense knowledge and expertise from their years in the field. The man who claims to have sold Patterson the suit lacks knowledge, experience, and proof. Why, then, should we listen to this man above the experts?

Another point that skeptics make to detract from the film is to question its quality. They tend to deride the film as grainy and shaky. They infer that this means that the film itself is of low quality. We will dive into both of these claims to determine their validity. We will discuss the latter first. The film is shaky, but that should not detract from the film. We would do well to remember that Patterson had a handheld camera without any supportive equipment. This means that any movement on Patterson's part would result in shaking. In fact, although his exact route is not known, we can make an educated guess about the path that Patterson took while filming. From his start-to-end point, he would have had to have run a considerable distance in a short time. The resultant shakiness should thus not detract from the film. A dynamic camera is the term used to refer to the camera's movement. In order to get a clear image, an entire team must keep the camera from shaking.[31] In fact, we would expect to see an unsteady camera when operated by a moving operator without any support for the camera.[32] The fact that the camera moves strengthens the argument that Patterson had to move to get into position as he filmed Patty during the look-back sequence. Indeed, had he hoaxed the film, Patterson may perhaps have started filming in a more advantageous position. Therefore, calling the film shaky does nothing to delegitimize the film and instead shows that said claim is made by one who knows little of what transpired that day.

Skeptics often deride the quality of the PGF in an attempt to delegitimize it. We have already discussed the shakiness expected from a Kodak K-100 16 mm camera (i.e., the one used by Patterson).[33] That particular camera had a very small frame with which to view the picture and had to be held with two hands. Holding onto a camera while simultaneously tracking a moving object—which was being viewed from a tiny lens—sufficiently explains why the film is so shaky in the beginning. It also explains why the film stops shaking: Patterson stopped moving. We can infer that Patterson planted himself as he was confident enough that his position would allow him to capture the best possible footage. Moreover, this also dispels the notion that Patterson intentionally shook the camera to hide flaws as we know that he was moving at the beginning of the film and that he captured the clearest, steadiest part of the film during the aforementioned worst-case scenario—Patty's head movement.

As we have discussed in detail, skeptics make claims that (they believe) delegitimize the PGF. However, upon closer inspection, these claims have a tendency to fall flat. Reiterating what we have said about the film location, filmmakers will cheat locations to make their jobs easier. Patterson did not do so when he made the long drive south to Bluff Creek. He also did not make life easier for himself by chasing after Patty. There are two frames that show Patterson approaching a creek. Looking at the layout of Patterson and Patty, we know that Patterson ran through the creek to get a better shot of Patty.[34] This may seem harmless, but it has significant implications. Why would Patterson do this to himself? Filming a man in an ape suit over 400 miles from home would have been hard enough. Adding in the extra challenge of trudging through a creek defies logic itself—especially because Patterson was wearing cowboy boots when he filmed Patty. Cowboy boots have poor traction at best and Patterson could have easily slipped in the water. Had this happened, all of his efforts would have been in vain. The camera would have been ruined, and all the time spent prepping the actor and suit would have been for naught.

It is fair to infer that, as technology advances, we would be better able to analyze the film. Indeed, thanks to Munns, we have access to high-quality images of the film that have only recently been made available. It is interesting to note that the use of modern technology to analyze the film has failed to provide any evidence of a hoax. Instead, it actually helps validate the film's authenticity. As discussed above, we can see the triceps, breasts, the back of Patty's neck after the head turn, and the muscle herniation in the quad, thanks to modern analysis. Another crucial aspect of the film is that it shows us the midtarsal break. In humans, the midtarsal bones are fused together to form an arch, not so in apes. Indeed, they provide an ape's foot with a flexibility not seen in humans. An ape the size of a Sasquatch, although bipedal, would need a specialized walking motion. The walking motion evident in the film is called a compliant gait. A compliant gait is a form of walking that relies on the individual not locking their legs when walking. Humans pole vault one leg over the other. However, an ape the size of a Sasquatch would not be able to walk like this as the stress placed on the lower joints would significantly damage them over time. Having a flexible foot is additionally beneficial in that it would reduce the stress placed on the foot by allowing a smoother transfer of weight (as compared to human feet). We can see in frames 310, 311, and 329 (see picture index) that the foot is bent in a manner impossible to replicate with the human foot. This marks another anatomically correct detail that could not have been faked.

During the creation of CGI figures, the initial phase involves sketching the character. Creating CGI figures is a difficult, time-consuming, and expensive process. We can assume that, if Patterson had hoaxed the film, he would have sketched a Sasquatch first as a prototype for his suit. Knowing what we know about prototypes in movie-making, we can safely assume that Patterson would have had to do the same. We can assume this because we know that Patty is at a caliber far above anything the best movie special effects crews could produce. We happen to have access to some figures that Patterson drew, which appear in his book. Interestingly, Patterson's own sketches do not match Patty. Comparing Figures 10 and 11 in the picture index, we can see that Patterson did not have an understanding of the biomechanics involved with the ape's foot as he simply sketched an enlarged human foot.

> The heel would have to extend further back from the ankle. The Patterson film clearly shows the creature's projecting heel-an esoteric biomechanical detail that no former rodeo rider bent on a hoax could have expected to know.[35]

Furthermore, the shape of the neck and the overall muscles do not match. Neither do the lengths of the limbs—specifically the legs. Examining Figure 10, we see that Patterson actually placed the sketched foot incorrectly. The ankle would have to have been shifted forward in order for an animal of this size to walk properly. We can see from the PGF that Patty has an ankle shifted forward in the exact way required to support her massive frame. One last point regarding Patterson's drawings. All but three of his sketches show male Sasquatches. This means that 84.2% of the Sasquatch sketches in his book are of males. It should be noted that Roger did not specifically say that each of the sketches were males, but we can safely assume so because he went out of his way to draw breasts on the females. The percentages tell us that Roger would have used a male Sasquatch to hoax the event because he was accustomed to drawing them.

A common argument made against Patterson comes in the form of his supposedly questionable reputation. This is used as a premise to the claim that Patterson hoaxed the film, yet such a premise does not support that conclusion. It is instead no more than an attack on his character. Such ad hominem attacks have become sadly common in our modern society. Even if Patterson's reputation were questionable because of an outstanding police warrant, that would not necessarily affect the authenticity of the film. In fact, we have seen before how making a suit of Patty's caliber was impossible. There was no legitimate way to make Patty. The only way Patterson could have filmed her is through her existence being real. Assuming Patterson had a poor reputation, one would have to explain exactly how that has any bearing upon the film. The quality of Patterson's character is irrelevant when the facts of the film are examined. Attacking a person's character does nothing to hurt their argument. Read any argument against the PGF and you will undoubtedly come across an attack on Patterson's character.

One person who refrains from this method is David Daegling. Daegling is the author of *Bigfoot Exposed: An Anthropologist Examines America's Enduring Legend*. We will here discuss his considerable amount of information and opinions on the PGF. Daegling admits that weak arguments made about Patty looking like an actor in a suit does nothing to disprove the PGF.[36] This statement is true as one could easily counter that the suit looks like a real animal. Neither of those arguments has any weight, so there is no need to discuss the faulty argument style used here. Before we begin to analyze Daegling's argument, we should note that he did exactly what believers want from scientists: he investigated the Sasquatch phenomenon. Granted, his conclusions stand in opposition to what believers would want to see, but nonetheless, we should commend him for taking the time to explore the existence of Sasquatches.

Daegling begins and ends his chapter on the PGF by stating that Patterson's drawings are an exemplar of what we see in the film. He says this on page 107 and continues by saying that "Someone did not need to dream up a costume, the template for the movie became publicly available in 1966."[37] Daegling is here inferring that Patterson used the drawings from his 1966 book as the basis for Patty's design. However, we can pose serious questions to Daegling's argument. Why did Patterson make a female suit? Most of his drawings were of male Sasquatches, meaning that he was more familiar with their anatomy. Next, why does the female Sasquatch with the most resemblance to Patty have such an anatomically different foot? The foot in his drawing is clearly just an enlarged human foot. However, Patty's foot has a heel that extends further back than on a human foot—a trait Dr. Grover Krantz says would be vital for such a large animal to walk bipedally. Dr. Jeff Meldrum agrees with this point.[38] Daegling argues against Krantz's heel argument by claiming that the shape of the heel does not make sense from a biomechanical perspective. He argues that there would be no benefit to a lengthened heel bone as the Achilles tendon would be attached too far forward. This may sound like a reasonable counter to Krantz, but it is rather difficult to see what Daegling is referring to as we do not have a clear view of the placement of the Achilles tendon. Additionally, we should note that, assuming Daegling is referring to the left heel (which is off the ground), the Achilles tendon could potentially look different from what Daegling would expect to see when the foot is not on firm ground. It could be said that Daegling has made some assumptions about the film, which cannot be properly inferred due to the angle of the foot.

Daegling argues that the extended heel exemplifies the fact that Patterson must have used a piece of a prosthetic foot device for the creation of his suit.[39] Although this seems like a reasonable explanation, it is weakened when we look at 1976's *King Kong*. The Kong suit, according to Daegling, would need an extended heel. There are brief clips that show this is not the case: when we first see Kong pick up Jessica Lang, the first part of the fight scene with the giant snake, and at the beginning of the scene where Kong is atop the twin towers. Daegling infers that the extended heel is meant to make it look "as if it is something else."[40] It is not entirely clear what this "something else" refers to. It seems highly improbable that Patterson would create a suit that perfectly mimics the anatomical features of an ape only to intentionally create a fake detail in the foot. Daegling's argument becomes even more questionable when we attempt to rationalize the so-called prosthetic foot. Walking while wearing a suit is challenging due to the weight of the suit and the constraints upon the actor's breathing and vision. A foot prosthetic would have made a difficult job that much harder. Furthermore, we know from Munns's frames that the foot can be seen bending in such a way as would have been impossible with the use of a prosthetic. Knowing all of this, we can safely discount Daegling's assumption that the foot is a prosthetic piece.

Daegling makes the claim that Patterson's drawings represent a possible model he used for the Patty suit. However, the significant anatomical (and, indeed, gender) differences between Patty and the sketches detract from this argument. Daegling does admit that Patty should be considered a realistic suit. Indeed, he acknowledges that there are certain anatomical details that we can see:

> The dynamics of the movement correspond to what we expect to see in a living flesh and blood biped. This observation does not really extract the film from the realm of hoax, however. It may simply mean that if this was a costume, it was a pretty good one.[41]

Daegling details that spandex was not available for use at this time, nor does he believe we should consider gluing hair onto the body of an actor a viable option. He does, however, list two ways in which he believes the Sasquatch could have been replicated. He says that placing bags of water beneath the skin of an extremely tight suit could recreate what we see in the PGF. While this is certainly an imaginative solution, it can be dismissed with one simple question: if such a high-quality suit could have been so easily made, why then did Hollywood not employ this technique? In fact, Daegling himself notes that "skeptics must deal with this fact of the film, it does not portray a poorly fashioned suit."[42] We know from sources that Patterson "had virtually no financial resources at the time."[43] We can then infer that the Patty suit was relatively cheap to make. If it was cheap and easy enough for an inexperienced amateur to make, why would Hollywood not have followed suit? If Hollywood had the ability, then why is there an absence of Patty-like suits on the big screen? Simple, Hollywood did not possess this ability, and neither did Patterson. Remember, *Planet of the Apes* had a budget of $1 million. It would be inconceivable to think that Hollywood would have spent that amount of money when Patterson had found an effective way to make a significantly more realistic suit at a fraction of the cost.

After investigating the film, Daegling learned that humans can replicate the look and speed of Patty's gait. While humans can indeed do this, it comes at a heavy physical cost. The energy required to walk in the way shown in the film would be immense. Without a suit, walking in Patty's manner would exhaust a person after one or two minutes. If a person in regular circumstances would be immediately exhausted, how quickly would it take a person in an ape suit to become severely fatigued? Especially an actor within the suit without an easy way to remove it. Taking an ape suit off takes time, which poses a serious risk to the (likely dehydrated) actor inside it. This further weakens Daegling's overall inference that Patty is a man in an ape suit. While Daegling should be commended for investigating the existence of Sasquatches the arguments contained therein do not stand up to scrutiny. Using what we know from the information presented in this chapter allows us to weaken the case for the PGF being hoaxed and instead strengthens the claim for its authenticity.

Hollywood has one true objective: to make money. They would have happily opened their arms to this Washington cowboy had he possessed the ability to create a cheap, realistic ape suit. Look no further than *Planet of the Apes*. John Chambers had as many as 80 makeup artists working for him on the film, each making approximately $1,200 to $1,400 a week, with an overall budget of $1 million (in 1967's money).[44] Needless to say, they would have happily employed Patterson or adopted his ideas in order to save themselves a significant amount of money. Furthermore, Patterson would have been rewarded for his efforts, which makes it all the more mystifying as to why he took his unique ape suit technique to the grave. One would think that Patterson, who died in 1972 of Hodgkin's lymphoma, would have come clean before his passing.[45] Someone close to Patterson said that he "had virtually no financial resources at the time."[46] Approaching death, Patterson chose not to sell his master technique to Hollywood in order to be able to leave money behind for his soon-to-be widowed wife and children; instead, he (inexplicably) took the secret to his grave.

As for the blurriness and the graininess of the video, we have to understand each of these aspects before we discuss their relation to the film. We have to remember that the film was shot in 1967. Our familiarity with 4K filming on the movies and TV shows that we watch makes us occasionally forget that 4K and UHD technology is a recent advancement. The film was shot in a time when film camera technology was still relatively simple, especially when compared to modern standards. Accordingly, is it fair to describe the film as high quality for its time? We see other movies from this era with a much clearer picture and with more vibrant colors. However, those cameras were not designed to be operated by someone while moving. The movie cameras of the time were meant to be stationary. That means that the engineering of both will be different. Designing a handheld film camera means that a high-quality image must be sacrificed in order to make it light enough to carry.

As for those who claim that the film is grainy, they are mistaken. "In film, it [grain] is caused by uneven distribution and variations in the size of film grain."[47] Noise can be limited if a director controls the environment: lighting, focus, and stability all factor into that equation. In a chance encounter, one cannot possibly control for the factors that would result in the highest quality film. We are spoiled today because teams of professional photographers will spend days, weeks, or even months, filming a specific animal. They then edit out any bad quality film and only show the highest quality pieces they captured, all while using some of the best photographic equipment available today. In so doing, they lull people into a false belief that taking photographs of wild animals is easy and always results in high-quality film.

> Why is the PGF so often called "grainy" when it is not? The actual likely cause for this belittling of the image quality is the fact that most people don't look at true full-frame images. If you saw a true full-frame image of a sharp frame (no motion blur), you would see it is very high-quality and not "grainy" at all. But most people simply look at the highly magnified images of the subject "creature," and that subject was generally not more than 1/6th of the frame height at its closest. So the magnification to make an image of just the film subject is a 6x magnification larger than what the film was intended to be viewed at, so you are seeing the film's grain magnified 6 times. Under those conditions, yes, you would see the grain with any film, not just this one.
>
> So the "grainy" description is incorrect in the true film sense but still widely used to disparage the film and suggest there's no precise image date to analyse.[48]

Claiming that the film is grainy is inaccurate. The fact is that the film was shot in 1967 and it was zoomed in six times the normal amount. Needless to say, the graininess of the film, which skeptics point to as proving its low quality, is actually false. Furthermore, if one did an analysis with Patty zoomed in, and they use a copy of the original film, then there is the possibility that they were analyzing something that may not have been in the original film or that the image lost clarity, which would present more potential areas of disparity among those who make arguments against the PGF.[49]

One theory has emerged that states that the PGF was actually a film that depicted a massacre of Sasquatches in their habitat. However, this claim is false as the flash that some believe to be from a gun was not contained within the original reel.

> One of the cornerstones of this was a white flare-like spec on the film, at frame 613, on one of John Green's copies. But it was apparently scanned for TV viewing and the TV conversion to 30 frames per second blended some frames and one such frame blend made a half intensity flare. Analysts thought they were seeing a gun muzzle flash increase and then disappear, but all they were really looking at was a single light flare on one copy, and the flare wasn't on any other copy, so it wasn't on the original film.[50]

This goes to show that Munns's analysis deserves to be viewed in a positive light as he has access to the largest and clearest images that exist of the PGF. Furthermore, Munns's analysis shows him to be ready to debunk any bad argument made about the PGF, whether from skeptics or believers. This means that we have strong grounds to consider his the most accurate analysis. Others who do not have access to the same images might, in fact, be arguing against something not evident in the original film. As for the quality, the later the generation of the film copy, the worse the quality will become.

There are certain arguments that sound reasonable until they are scrutinized. Some argue that we should eliminate carbon emissions from our economy to help prevent climate change. A cleaner environment is, after all, something we all want. However, eliminating carbon emissions without a suitable alternative would destroy the economy of every country around the world that enacted said elimination and result in a mass international exodus. Similarly, claiming Patterson hoaxed the PGF sounds reasonable at face value. Of course, Sasquatches cannot possibly exist, so the PGF must obviously be a hoax. And yet, under the scrutiny contained within this chapter, you can see how the above argument is fallacious. In fact, claiming that Patty was a member of a real species is a much less preposterous claim than the notion that Patterson hoaxed the event. Patterson hoaxing the event defies common sense. How so, you may still ask. Well, Hollywood's most talented could not have created a suit of the same caliber as Patty. Patty's anatomical features are consistent with other apes, whereas the suits made by movie special effects teams are not. The film location would have been less than ideal for a hoax, as would running through the creek while holding specialist equipment. Everything listed in this chapter is an empirical fact that can easily be verified with a minimum amount of searching. You can decide for yourself what the implications of this chapter are.

2

THE MYAKKA APE PHOTOS

The PGF has received a significant amount of well-deserved attention from researchers due to its being the most compelling piece of evidence for the existence of Sasquatch. Although it deserves the attention it gets, it also detracts from other pieces of evidence. There are many photos of Sasquatches, most of questionable quality, that have not received this same level of attention. There is only one other set of photographic evidence that can be placed alongside the PGF in terms of quality. These are called the Myakka Ape Photos. Unlike the PGF, which comes in video form, the Myakka Ape Photos come in the form of two photographs. At first glance, much like the PGF, it is questionable whether the figure is a Sasquatch. Upon further inspection, one is left with little doubt as to what the photo shows.

In the early 2000s, near the Myakka State Forest in Florida, an elderly woman kept experiencing an issue on her property. She noticed that someone kept stealing apples from her yard. This happened time and time again. Naturally, the woman wanted to know what was happening to her apples. It just so happened that one night, she heard a noise in her backyard. She wanted to catch the culprit red-handed, so she headed outside, with her camera at the ready. The woman, with her flash on, captured two photos. To her surprise, she captured a photograph of an uninvited guest: not just to her backyard but also to the Florida ecosystem. Many of those who saw the photograph believed it to be of an orangutan.

What is an orangutan, an ape species native to Sumatra and Borneo, doing in this elderly woman's backyard? This question is what warranted an investigation into these two photos. To more ably determine the type of ape in the photos, we must first better understand the anatomy of an orangutan. Orangutans, as we have said, are native to Sumatra or Borneo. Unlike other great apes, such as gorillas and chimps, orangutans are solitary animals. They tend to live their lives in relative isolation, broken only by territorial disputes, mating, and a female ape caring for her infant. As for their anatomy, orangutans are arboreal animals, meaning that they have exceptionally long arms.[1] Although they have long arms, they have rather short legs. They need long, strong arms to be able to climb trees and support their bodies. In fact, they are the largest arboreal animal in the world. This explains both the strength of their arms and the shortness of their legs. They rarely walk on the forest floor due to their short legs and, when they do, they are rather slow.

The flash of the elderly woman's camera seemed to have startled the ape. Needless to say, the ape was not expecting to see such bright lights at so late an hour. The expression on the face of the ape says it all. The ape bared its teeth at the woman, most likely as a warning. However, the woman did not leave, so the ape resorted to another intimidation display, albeit one that helps identify the ape. It stood erect, perhaps not fully (we can see it is slightly hunched in the second photo), but its overall size appears immense. This time, the intimidation worked, and the sight of an ape of monstrous proportions was enough to send the woman fleeing back into to her house.

Standing fully erect seems like a natural display to this ape. Bears do the same thing to show off their size. Cats puff themselves up to make it look like they are larger than they actually are. The same can be said of puff adders, which get their name due to their habit of puffing themselves up to ward off potential predators. As an animal, showing off your size is an effective way to stop a potential confrontation before it begins. The behavior displayed by the Myakka ape is exactly what we would expect from an animal startled by the flash of the camera. Indeed, the ape's intimidating behavior was extremely successful.

The Myakka ape left us an exceptionally important clue to its identity: it stood upright. Orangutans are certainly not native to Florida. This is not to say that there are none living in Florida. There are many plausible explanations as to how an orangutan could have made it to Florida: escaping from a zoo or circus or being released into the wild by a private owner. However, the Myakka ape is not an orangutan. I concede that the ape shares extreme similarities with orangutans. There is one thing that makes it impossible for the ape to have been an orangutan. It is physically impossible for an orangutan to stand to the height of the Myakka ape. Orangutans have short legs and are, overall, very short apes.

The woman estimated that the figure was between six and a half to seven feet tall. Orangutans grow to a maximum of approximately five feet. There are two possible explanations for the woman's estimate that we will examine: the woman was incorrect in that she either over-or underestimated its height (we shall also briefly discuss estimation in this possibility as well). We will look at both possibilities. First, the woman who took the photos was elderly. As an elderly individual, there is a chance she suffered from some sort of ailment that caused a decline in her mental fortitude. However, the woman wrote a well-written and completely coherent note to the local police department expressing concern over the incident. Writing a note to the proper authorities expressing concern over the incident means that it was unlikely she was suffering from severe cognitive decline. Accordingly, the woman's cognitive ability should not be in question.

As an elderly woman, we can safely assume that she has encountered many people in her life. As such, we can further confidently assume that she would be able to make a somewhat accurate estimation of the figure's height. Let us assume she did overestimate, we have to ask ourselves by how much? Perhaps the figure was only five and a half to six feet tall. That would still make the ape taller than the tallest orangutans. It should be noted that this "orangutan" would be living in a non-native habitat. Animals in non-native habitats can thrive—albeit at the cost of native animals—but when they do, there is usually a breeding population. As there were no other reports of orangutans in the area, it would be safe to infer the absence of a breeding population in Florida. We can also eliminate the fact that the woman overestimated the height as the ape did not stand fully erect. The figure was slightly hunched, meaning that it is likely the figure would have been at least 12 inches taller, meaning that it would stand at least seven feet tall. We should seriously consider whether the woman underestimated the height of the figure. Looking at the second photo, we can see that the figure is extremely tall, even when not fully upright. Standing at a height the woman estimated would put the figure approximately 30% taller than orangutans are known to grow.

Another detail that casts doubt over the claim that the photos depict an orangutan is that, being a seclusive, arboreal animal, why this ape would approach this woman's property. Orangutans prefer to be left alone and are naturally afraid of humans. Why would this orangutan approach the woman's property? You can claim that the ape was an escaped animal raised in captivity. This claim seems legitimate. However, if the orangutan was used to being around humans, we would expect to hear more reports of encounters with this animal. At the time of writing, there have been no reports of anyone sighting an orangutan in or around this area. This implies that the Myakka ape was not raised in captivity, thereby casting further doubt over this ape being an orangutan. No orangutan would risk exposing themselves just to get apples unless, of course, escape was easy. However, the ape's first response was not to escape, and its hesitancy in doing so allowed an elderly woman to take two photographs.

There are some questions surrounding the PGF. We have

discussed how these do little to delegitimize the film, but, nonetheless, these questions do exist. There are few, if any, questions that exist with the Myakka ape photos. We have an ape that, at first glance, appears to be an orangutan. However, the case immediately complexifies. The ape is taller than the tallest orangutans by a considerable margin, and it approached the woman's house in a manner no orangutan would. The ape could not have been an orangutan. If not an orangutan, then what is it? Let me reword that question. What is more likely: the ape in the photo is an orangutan that grew significantly larger than normal, or the photos are evidence that points to the existence of a species of unknown hominoid(s) living in North America?

3

FOOTPRINTS

While teaching second grade in an inner-city school in Milwaukee, I was exposed to many new things. Indeed, growing up in an unincorporated town meant that moving to Milwaukee was more than just a culture shock. Back when in high school, there were many days when I would get caught behind a tractor or some other kind of farm equipment. Driving during the fall was also eventful as the deer began to move the closer it got to their mating season. Needless to say, there were not many tractors or deer in Milwaukee.

What Milwaukee does have is people—a lot of them. Highly populous areas typically mean a mix of different cultures. The culture of the area I taught in was so different from where I had gone to school, which is exactly what made the experience worthwhile. Exposure to this area and such a vast array of cultures taught me many things. One of the most interesting of which I learned happened to come from a kids book. During our read-aloud time, we covered many subjects. Most of these were books that taught the children important moral lessons: work hard, do not make fun of others, do the right thing, etc. One thing that really stuck in my mind was a fact from a book about the moon.

The moon is more fascinating than I feel most of us give it credit for. While the Earth itself is vastly different from most other planets, the moon is almost exponentially different from Earth. There is one difference between the Earth and the moon that especially caught my attention: footprints left by astronauts on the moon will last indefinitely. Think of how astonishing that is. Reaching the moon in the first place was amazing enough. Now consider that part of the proof that they were there could potentially stay there forever. No wind or rain will ever erode the footprints. As long as nothing disturbs the paths these astronauts trod, their footprints will last as long as the moon itself.

This truly reminded me about how special living on Earth is. Not only is our existence finite, so too would the evidence for it be were it not for our complex technological advancements that allow us to record virtually every aspect of our lives. The permanence of the evidence of the astronauts walking on the moon is like nothing we have on our planet. Walking on the beach near the water is enough to erase the evidence of your footprints almost as soon as they are left in the sand.

Animals also leave traces of themselves in an area. Much like footprints in the sand, these signs last a finite time. However, although it seems that footprints are only snapshots of something walking through an area, they provide us with a wealth of information. One can determine the species, size, and number of animals in a group based on footprints alone. As such, they are far more complex than they appear at first sight.

Footprints are one of the most vital pieces of information that help conservationists find elusive animals. Usually, an animal is elusive due to a relatively small population. There are other aspects to consider, but this tends to generally be the case. When people search for elusive animals, they must first find some kind of evidence for their existence. The two forms of evidence that most help conservationists are either footprints or sightings. Sighting an elusive animal means that you were in the right place at the right time to encounter one. Finding a footprint is a different story. You do not need to be as lucky to find a footprint as you do to have an encounter. All that is required is to walk in the same path as that of one of these animals. Hopefully, the conditions are conducive for both the foot of the animal to imprint in the ground and for the print to be preserved for as long as possible. Just one single footprint can be enough for conservationists to begin conducting their research in an area.

There are two elusive animals that are worth discussing here: the Siberian tiger and the Knysna elephant (the southernmost elephant in the world). Both animals required an enormous amount of careful work by experts in order to be found. First, we will talk about the Siberian tiger. Tigers truly are the perfect predators. Their size, strength, camouflage, and intelligence make them one of the fiercest animals alive today. Failing to take the proper safety precautions when dealing with these deadly cats would likely lead to one's death. We are all too lucky not to have tigers in North America, we would be prevented from continuing many of our outdoor activities.

Sooyong Park is highly experienced in dealing with these beautiful but deadly cats. His goal was simple: to film them in their own habitats. Siberian tigers live in extremely harsh conditions. The tigers are also highly skittish of humans, rarely allowing themselves to be seen. As such, they are one of the most elusive animals in the world. Tigers are also known to travel vast distances in short periods of time—further complicating the act of finding one. It is no wonder that, before Park set out on his journey, there was less than an hour's worth of footage of these felines.[1] Setting up in the tiger's known territory affords researchers the possibility of actually finding one of these creatures. Park and his team would spend days looking for footprints.[2] In fact, the tigers were so cautious of humans that they would avoid being seen in the area.[3] This made it that much more important to be able to locate their tracks.

There are many difficulties with tracking wild animals. Both the terrain and weather are challenges to be overcome. The animals themselves—especially large animals like tigers—represent the biggest danger. Researchers' goal when tracking large animals is to get close enough to study them. Naturally, this is highly dangerous when it comes to tigers due to their capability of killing a person quickly. Getting close to one is a great way to get the data one wants, but it is also a highly effective way of, literally, entering the jaws of death.

The large size of the tiger's territory makes locating them even more difficult. The fact that their food migrates throughout the year is a further challenge. Common sense would dictate that following the food would be relatively easy and that doing so would increase the odds of finding the tigers. However, the eating habits of the tigers' prey vary from year to year.[4] It is no wonder tigers are so elusive. The researchers who seek them have very little in their favor.

Park was eventually able to capture the footage he wanted. He spent almost a decade of his life in a tiny bunker in the Siberian wilderness with his camera pointed out of the window to get photos and videos of these tigers. Despite the elusiveness of the tigers, setting up camp in such a location made it possible to capture the footage as the area contained tiger tracks and other signs. Without having found these tracks and making use of knowledge from the locals, Park's quest would have been unsuccessful.

Gareth Patterson's story shares many similarities with Park. Like Park, Patterson worked with big cats. Specifically, Patterson spent many years working with lions. However, something occurring to a different species caught his attention. He heard of an elephant species near extinction. Indeed, there were some who believed that the Knysna elephants were already extinct. Patterson decided to venture out in search of these exceptionally large yet elusive animals.

Searching for elusive animals is highly challenging. However, one might be forgiven for assuming that searching for elephants would be relatively easier compared to smaller animals. After all, elephants are huge, so it would be very difficult to miss one, or so one would think. Once one enters a forested region, such as the Knysna forest, many realizations begin to dawn: none bigger than the fact that forests expertly hide even the largest of animals. Indeed, when talking to a forest worker about the elephants, Patterson asked how a young bull was able to avoid detection for 20 years. The explanation given to him was simple: "The forests are very big... And though elephants are huge, the forests make them small in comparison."[5] Forests have the tendency to make large animals look small. They also are known for concealing large animals due to how thick the foliage can be.

Enter Patterson. Patterson was no stranger to conservation due to his work with lions, but his elephant search would be fruitful in many unimaginable ways (which we shall fully explore in a later chapter). As Patterson's search began, he would soon come to realize that his search for elephants would present more questions than answers. He began his journey by collecting information so as to best prepare himself for the challenges ahead. He knew that entering the thick, forested regions where the elephants were rumored to live without sufficient knowledge would be unwise. As he prepared his expedition, it was clear that he would need the freedom to work solely and tirelessly at his goal of uncovering the secrets of these rarely seen elephants. His research was self-funded. There are pros and cons to self-funding an expedition: The most significant pro is that it affords one the freedom to focus on whatever one chooses, the biggest con is that it tends to drain one's financial resources.

Patterson was up to the task of finding these extremely rare elephants. Of course, as stated above, he did not go in blind. Patterson learned the land in order to increase his odds and also learned to search for the correct signs of an elephant's presence in an area.[6] Some of the locals provided useful information for the whereabouts of these elephants; others were less amenable. There were some who believed that the population of the elephants was so low that they gave up hope in either finding or saving them.[7] Indeed, the elephants are so elusive, and the forests so thick, that very little is known of these elephants.[8]

The search began for Patterson as he began combing the Knysna forests for signs of these elephants. Within his first month, Patterson hit gold: he found droppings.[9] Finding droppings or other signs can reveal three salient facts about an animal: where it came from, where it was at the time of the droppings, and where it was going. Following this particular elephant's direction allowed Patterson to find other signs, such as footprints.[10] This was a highly fortunate find by Patterson, and his search was validated early on because of it. However, it would take Patterson a considerably longer time to actually see an elephant.

Finding a footprint of an elusive animal can be a bittersweet experience. You would naturally feel elated that the animal is alive and has recently passed through the area. And yet, it is also natural to feel somewhat dejected as you have just missed an opportunity to see the animal. You might think that Patterson would have seen the elephants almost immediately, especially considering that he found a trail within his first month. Indeed, this seems reasonable, but elusive animals typically live up to their name. By the time Patterson's book was published (*The Secret Elephants: The Rediscovery of the World's Most Southerly Elephants*) in 2009, he had spent over six years searching for elephants and had not had a sighting in years. Patterson knew from the signs that they were in the Knysna forest, but it still took him over three years to finally have a visual sighting of one of these elephants.[11] Before this, Patterson had only had quick glimpses which passed so quickly it was as if a sighting had never actually occurred.

There are some strong similarities between Park and Patterson. First, they both searched for elusive animals of which little was known. Notice that serious sacrifices by credible scientists were needed in order to unravel the mystery of these elusive creatures. Park spent 10 years (over a 20 year period) looking for tigers, and Patterson—while writing his first book on elephants—spent 6 (he would go on to devote much more time after the book's publication). Many people are ignorant of the process of searching for elusive animals as they assume it to be as simple and easy as strolling into a forest and taking a few pictures. Park and Patterson proved that this was certainly not the case. Finding and photographing the animals was not the first step in the process. Instead, extensive data had to be collected. They had to look for signs and anything at all that would help them shed light on these mysterious animals. Usually, they found footprints that determined an area in which these animals had traveled through before. However, the animals lived on large tracts of land so, even if one finds a sign of them being in an area, it does not guarantee that the animal will be found.

For those searching for elusive animals, tracks are the perfect pieces of evidence as they indicate the animal's presence (either past or current) in an area and help point the researcher in the right direction. Consider that, "An animal only has one skeleton, but can leave millions of tracks."[12] Finding an elusive animal is no easy task, as evidenced by the stories above. Finding the body of a recently deceased elusive animal, which has yet to be decomposed, is that much harder. Elusive animals are elusive for many reasons, one of those being that they live in thickly forested areas. Such areas complicate finding these animals while alive, and even more so once dead. Animals know when they are not feeling well, and they tend to relocate to areas in which they feel is safe. These areas are not easy to find. If they were, these sick animals would be easy pickings for predators. When it passes, an elusive animal will only leave behind one body: which will decay beyond recognition in a surprisingly short amount of time.

All of this means that looking for tracks is arguably the most effective way to learn about elusive animals—including their territory. As for what animal left a particular track, this requires specialist knowledge:

> Identifying what animals made which particular track is relatively straightforward. You compare the shape of the hands and feet... by following this checklist, you can usually figure out which general group of animals left the track.[13]

When Park and Patterson examined the tiger and elephant tracks, respectively, they were easily able to identify what had left them. Patterson had the easier task of identifying an elephant track (no other animal in the forest could leave such large tracks). Tiger tracks are rather more complicated to correctly identify as they share many similarities between canines.

For the average person, determining the difference between canine and tiger prints is easier said than done. However, for Park, it was a relatively straightforward task. Tigers do not leave claw marks, their paws are significantly larger, and their toes are in different positions. Needless to say, we should trust experts when they tell us which track belongs to which animal. Accordingly, what should we do when we have experts in a field telling us that there is evidence of an unidentified ape roaming the woods of North America? By experts, I, of course, mean those who actually study the evidence, not those who dismiss it out of hand or those who simply proffer their own conjecture. Two noteworthy anthropologists tasked themselves with solving the mystery of these large footprints left across North America: Drs. Grover Krantz and Jeff Meldrum. Although Dr. Krantz passed away, his contribution to the field still lives on.

Dr. Krantz, like most Americans, did not believe in the existence of Sasquatches. However, he felt that he needed to investigate the evidence with which he was presented as an obligation all scientists must adhere to: that of always seeking the truth. Dr. Krantz, as we said, was skeptical of Sasquatch stories and considered the evidence through this same dubious mindset. To his surprise, after examining a print that showed extensive deformities, he came to the conclusion that there was only one possible explanation: a biologically real ape left the print.[14] The print is known as "Cripplefoot" due to the deformities present. John Napier is exceptionally skeptical of Sasquatch in his book. However skeptically he writes, even Napier concedes that the print would have been beyond the technical capability of a hoaxer.

> It is difficult to conceive of a hoaxer so subtle, so knowledgeable—and so sick—who would deliberately fake a footprint of this nature. I suppose it is possible, but it is so unlikely that I am prepared to discount it.[15]

This particular print was cast in Washington in late 1969.[16] The tracks show evidence of an injury that resulted in a severely deformed foot. That same foot left no doubt in Dr. Krantz's mind of the existence of Sasquatches.[17]

Skeptics overlook footprint casts. As discussed above, they offer far more information than the average layperson would believe. Many assume that footprint casts are similar to cameras in the sense that they represent a photo of where an animal (or a hoaxer, as a skeptic would argue) trod. However, that would be understating the importance of leaving a print. A print is less like a photo and more like a GIF. Footprints can best be described as "not a static mold of the foot, but rather a record of transient dynamic interaction of the foot with the ground."[18] The dynamic interaction of the foot with the ground is why footprints are best compared to non-motionless GIFs.

There is an additional advantage that helps experts determine whether or not a print belongs to an ape: dermal ridges. Many of us will have all watched some type of TV show about criminal investigations. The seemingly impossible task of catching the criminal who committed a heinous act becomes that much harder when the perpetrator carefully made sure not to leave a trace behind. That is until the forensic team miraculously finds a salient clue that helps the team crack the case: a fingerprint. The same is happening in the woods of North America, albeit on a much less dramatized scale. There are large, man-like prints appearing all over North America, and we have little idea of what is leaving them. Luckily, a significant amount of prints have been cast using a type of plaster to make a copy of the print. This allows the experts to examine the prints, much like how forensic teams dust for fingerprints.

Drs. Krantz and Meldrum were both well equipped to examine these supposed Sasquatch footprint casts due to their academic backgrounds—much like Park and Patterson in relation to tigers and elephants. While examining the casts, both anthropologists noticed what appeared to be dermal ridges. Accepting that their knowledge in the field of dermatoglyphics was somewhat lacking, they sought the help of experts with the necessary requisite knowledge. We would do well to remember that those who studied the dermal ridges worked in the criminal justice field, and their word was enough to determine the guilt of a potential criminal. We should take this to mean that the word of these experts is of the utmost accuracy and reliability.

> These footprints casts have been examined in detail by the police experts in cities of Pullman, Stevenson, and Seattle in Washington; Davis, Oakland, San Francisco, San Jose, and San Diego in California; Cheyenne, Wyoming; Denver, Colorado; Salem, Oregon; and Vancouver, British Columbia. They have been studied by the top state investigators in Wyoming, Washington, and Kansas (by Robert Olson, Sr.). The current and former heads of fingerprinting at the F.B.I. have examined them, as have several experts each at the Smithsonian Institution and Scotland Yard. Cast copies or lifts have been sent to experts in Toronto (Ontario), London (England), Moscow (old U.S.S.R.), and Beijing (China). I have omitted most of the names of these authorities because the few I did make note of would only clutter these pages, and most of these people are too busy to be pestered with numerous inquiries.[19]

There was one expert, though, who was unwilling to say these prints were authentic. Why? Due to the fact that the implications of the tracks being genuine were too much for him to imagine.[20] Dr. Meldrum also asked for the opinions of more fingerprint experts. Jimmy Chilcutt, a forensic scientist who specialized in fingerprints, was asked to determine the legitimacy of the footprint casts' dermal ridges. Chilcutt was arguably the best person to do so due to his considerable experience in studying both ape and human dermal ridges. He did this to better understand the latter and hopefully learn something that could potentially reveal a more accurate method for understanding fingerprints in the future.

If anyone could shed light on this mystery, it was Chilcutt. Needless to say, he was shocked by what he found from examining the casts. He said, without a doubt, that the dermal ridges on the casts suggested the existence of an unidentified ape living in the woods of North America.[21] Furthermore, Chilcutt was willing to stake his reputation on such a claim. You may not believe in Sasquatches, but you must at least take the opinions of fingerprint experts seriously when they determine casts to be legitimate. As we will discuss later, people who publicly assert the existence of Sasquatches risk hurting their reputations and careers. Indeed, both Drs. Krantz and Meldrum had their careers damaged by declaring their interest in the subject. So when Chilcutt went on record, it was crucial to understanding the great risk to his reputation. Did the potential fifteen minutes of fame (from Chilcutt making so bold a claim) carry a greater potential reward than the risk incurred by showing interest in the subject of Sasquatches? Chilcutt, and many other experts, clearly had (and continue to have) more to lose from showing their interest.

To test that the dermal ridges were the byproduct of an ape instead of a chance occurrence from the plaster process, tests were conducted as to whether these ridges could have been replicated.

> This phenomenon was repeated experimentally in the lab with human footprints left in fine loess and cast. Similar patterns of ridge preservation were replicated. Under the extremely dry conditions of the fine loess, which tended to wick the water away from plaster quite rapidly, pouring artifacts were occasionally produced that superficially resembled thick parallel ridges. These artifacts did not consistently exhibit uniform width or other fine details characteristic of dermatoglyphics; nor could these conditions account for ridge detail in casts poured in wet slit or mud.[22]

Eliminating either a chance occurrence or human forgery adds credibility to the testimony of the fingerprint experts discussed in this chapter.

Another noteworthy feature that Chilcutt identified on these footprint casts were the scars. More specifically, he noticed that the dermal ridges on the casts healed toward the scar, which is exactly what happens in humans when an injury heals.[23] Another fingerprint expert was asked to inspect the prints to see if he could determine whether they were made by a hoaxer or a living animal. Edward Palmer was able to provide a definitive answer after his examination.

> He could not see how the patterns could have been patched together from smaller parts that were copied from skin of a known primate. Beyond the overall patterns, the detailed structure of the ridges conformed to real friction skin. The evident sweat pores were aligned and spaced as expected and distinct from the occasional bubble in the plaster. Finally, he concluded, "I began this investigation with the goal of showing how these prints were, or might have been, faked. All the evidence now tells me that any faking would be impossible."[24]

Palmer was left with no doubt that whatever had left the prints was a living animal hitherto unknown to science.[25] The more we delve into the opinions of the experts concerning the footprints found in the woods of North America, the more we can understand why that one expert chose not to comment on the casts. The implications of these findings were enormous. We trust these fingerprint experts to provide reliable evidence with which to determine a man's guilt, why then should we not trust them regarding the mystery that is the existence of Sasquatches?

The fingerprint experts who examined these prints had one thing in common: their word was either enough to vindicate or incriminate potential criminals. Their expertise would have been enough to build a case against a suspect. If their word is enough to build a case in a court of law, then what does that say about their opinions of these footprint casts? Furthermore, we should note that these experts were not Sasquatch researchers or enthusiasts—as is often claimed by skeptics so as to devalue their opinions. However, this is not the case. These were unbiased experts simply attempting to help solve a mystery. We know of their neutrality as they have not conducted any research into the subject, or, if they have, they have certainly not publicized it. Either way, they were simply asked to lend their expertise, and they happily obliged. As experts in their field, it is likely that they felt it was their obligation to help provide answers to a question that has stumped many people.

One last expert we should talk about is Benny Kling. As with the others discussed in this chapter, he was a fingerprint expert that examined the casts.

> Benny Kling, Law Enforcement Academy Instructor, Douglas, Wyoming, likewise examined inked latex lifts and the original casts and drew the same conclusion that the casts exhibited characteristics of real friction skin from a high primate. He added a note on the apparent mirrored symmetry of the right and left feet. He pointed out [a] breakdown of the smoothing of the ridges under weight-bearing areas, as might be expected of a living foot, are near mirror images; some dysplasia is indicated in the areas where it could be expected, smoothing by wear shows on the weight-bearing areas. In summary, he said, "This kind of print could not have been manufactured by a human foot, or that of any known animal. It could not have been manufactured by a hoaxer; the design is too dermatoglyphically correct, and the engraving job would be beyond the capabilities of the best forger."[26]

Notice how all of the experts who look at these prints, at a minimum, believe that it warrants an investigation. Most of them noted the potential knowledge stored within these prints.

Although the dermal ridges are a highly conducive piece of evidence in favor of the existence of Sasquatches, this is far from the only thing that we can ascertain from the prints. As stated earlier, the prints should not be thought of as static but more of a real-world GIF of the animal's foot, leaving an impression on the ground. We can learn a lot from an animal's gait just by examining a footprint. Outside of looking at the prints to determine the walking mechanics used to achieve it, we can also learn much from the size and shape of the footprints. One thing that we can ascertain from the prints as a whole is whether they are indicative of a living animal. As footprint casts move north, they become larger, which is what we would expect to see from an animal. "The reported size variations are real and apparently regular from south to north."[27] The footprints fit into our understanding of the natural world due to their following of Bergmann's Rule: which states that the further north an animal gets, the larger its body will grow. The larger an animal's body, the less heat it will lose to the cold as its surface area to volume ratio is reduced.[28]

Napier noted in his book that an anthropologist by the name of Don Abbott concluded it unlikely that a hoaxer fabricated the prints. "I find this possibility almost as incredible as that of the existence of the creature."[29] Indeed, Abbott continues with:

> The evidence that I have examined persuades me that some of the tracks are real, and that they are man-like in form. One might expect that having accepted these propositions one could pursue them painlessly to their logical conclusion-that they have been made by a man-like creature... the mind starts to boggle at such a preposterous idea. The vision of such creatures stomping barefoot through the forests of north-west America, unknown to science, is beyond common sense. Yet reason argues that this is the case.[30]

Abbott, here, follows the scientific process to a tee. He has preconceived notions about the existence of a bipedal ape in North America. However, he does not allow this to interfere with his interpretations of the evidence. Regardless of it defying common sense (or, more accurately, common belief), the evidence suggests that there is a bipedal ape in North America. While he knew the risks of saying so, he felt scientifically obliged to report what he felt was an accurate representation of the work and research he had conducted on the subject.

We have touched upon Bergmann's rule, but the footprints follow scientific rules that other animal populations follow as well. The prints are also uniform in their shape:

> There is a curious and persuasive consistency about the hourglass footprints. They present an aberrant but, nevertheless, uniform pattern. This is hard to reconcile with fakery. One might pose the question: who other than God or natural selection is sufficiently conversant with the subtleties of the human foot and the human walking style to 'design' an artificial foot which is so perfectly harmonious in terms of structure and function?[31]

The footprints that have been cast number close to a thousand, if not more. There have been many more that have been seen and photographed. "The question of existence remains open. But if even one set of yeti or sasquatch tracks were genuine..."[32] Even Napier concedes that the likelihood of all the footprints being fake is near zero.

> I am sure that *some* Sasquatch tracks are fakes, but it is beyond reason to suppose that they all are. Indeed if there was only one real print among 99 fakes it would be obligatory to explain the one.[33]

Many assume that because humans are bipedal, any other bipedal ape would display the same walking mechanics. However, there are some key indicators as to why this is false. Humans are not entirely covered in hair. From an evolutionary perspective, this means that early humans were most likely long-distance runners when they hunted prey. Not being covered in body hair would have allowed early humans to cool off more quickly. This means that they potentially ran animals to the point of exhaustion. Another fact that helps validate this is that the midtarsal bones fused together to form an arch in the human foot.

The implications of this are rather significant, despite most people being unaware of this fact. Indeed, it is fair to say that the few people who do know this are mostly anthropologists who would not waste their time leaving fake footprints in the woods of North America. Knowing this, it is safe to infer that hoaxers would not be capable of making an anatomically accurate foot as they would naturally (and erroneously) assume that they would only need to make an enlarged human foot. As such, it becomes quite the enigma when one finds prints in the woods of North America that appear similar to human feet. Luckily, we have Dr. Meldrum, who specializes in primate locomotion, to analyze these prints.

> Sasquatch footprints generally lack the indications of differential pressure beneath heel and ball as in an arched foot but instead are rather uniform in depth. Occasionally, the dynamic signature of the foot indicates a more apelike midfoot flexibility. In all, the sasquatch footprint is not merely an enlarged facsimile of a human footprint, but appears to represent a uniquely adapted primate foot associated with a distinctive mode of bipedalism.[34]

Meldrum continues this with:

> Their superficially human-like appearance is largely the consequence of the inner big toe being aligned with the remaining toes, whereas an ape's inner toe diverges much like a thumb. The resemblance to human footprints largely stops there, however. In fact, the sasquatch footprints lack the principal distinctive features that set the human foot apart from that of its hominoid cousins. Sasquatch footprints are typically flat with no consistent indications of the true hallmark of the human foot-affixed longitudinal arch. Additionally, there is little indication of differential weight bearing under a specialized "ball" at the base of the big toe. The sasquatch foot is relatively broader and the sole pad apparently thicker, by comparison to human feet. The heel and toe segments are disproportionately longer.[35]

Moreover, Meldrum was the first to understand that the pressure ridge evident in Sasquatch prints was due to the midtarsal break found within ape feet. Not even Dr. Krantz, with his decades of anthropological experience, noticed this. The reason for this is due to Dr. Meldrum specializing in this specific area of study. Does it seem at all likely that hoaxers would be able to fabricate and plant footprints so anatomically accurate that they could fool the likes of Drs. Krantz and Meldrum?

When a layperson happens upon a footprint in the woods that resembles a human's foot, only enlarged, they likely have questions. Indeed, so do the experts. The difference between them is that the experts have the knowledge to properly assess the prints' validity. When experts examine the prints, they find details available that would be unavailable to the layperson.

> ... the sasquatch foot retains the primitive apelike characteristic of a flat flexible midfoot. The range of motion permitted by the calcaneocuboid and

talonavicular joints allows the heel to function in leverage and propulsion somewhat independently of the relatively prehensile function of the forefoot. In primates, this coordinated flexion between the two segments of the foot is referred to as the "mid-tarsal break."[36]

It was not until Dr. Meldrum examined the prints that he discovered the midtarsal break evident in Sasquatch prints. We should note that prints with a midtarsal break were found at the PGF film site. How would Patterson, and other subsequent hoaxers, have known to include a pressure ridge on the fake tracks indicating a midtarsal break when said pressure ridges were previously unknown to the scientists who investigated them? These "hoaxers" should be commended for their extraordinary ability to fool everyone on this tiny detail for almost 50 years!

Returning to the PGF, David Daegling stated that the elongated heel was anatomically incorrect, meaning that Patterson must have used a foot prosthetic to build the Patty suit and prints. However, Dr. Meldrum refutes this claim.

This midfoot flexibility also explains the relatively elongated heel attributed to the sasquatch foot. Critics of the Patterson-Gimlin film took exception to a protruding heel that suggested to them oversized fake feet worn by a "man in a fur suit." One skeptic went so far as to assert that the Achilles tendon appeared to attach far forward on the heel in an unnatural fashion, negating any mechanical advantage afforded by the elongated heel. These explanations are simply based on erroneous interpretations of the appearance of the subject or blatant ignorance of foot mechanics.[37]

Dr. Krantz furthers this by saying:

> In my judgement, no hoaxer could have figured out just how far forward to shift the ankle for a biped of the indicated size, then have left footprints with some subtle distortions that just *might* lead an anatomist to the reconstruction I made. I figured the whole thing out after studying the footprints; any hoaxers had to plan it all out from nothing. This requires an expert anatomist with a very inventive mind, more so than me, and I seriously doubt that such person exists. And this does not take into account any of the other problems relating to how the tracks could have been planted.[38]

Not only does Dr. Krantz's argument weaken Daegling's criticism of the PGF, but it also detracts from the hoax hypothesis as a whole. How would any amateur have the knowledge to make an anatomically correct fake Sasquatch print? Dr. Krantz admits that even he, with all of his knowledge in the field of anthropology, could not have inferred these details without these prints. The two assumptions needed for the great ape hypothesis are that Sasquatches are real and live in North America. The hoax hypothesis would have to contain many more assumptions in order to present even a mediocre theory.

In a later chapter, we will list and discuss all of the assumptions that constitute the hoax hypothesis. As for a quick summary, the hoax hypothesis rests on the assumption that there is either a large team of hoaxers or a large number of individual hoaxers who are planting footprints in the woods of North America. Either assumption defies common sense and neither can properly explain the anatomical accuracy of the prints or how they can convince anthropologists and fingerprint experts alike. Needless to say, the consistency of the details and accuracy of these footprints serve as the repeatability requirement (necessary for the scientific process) within the study of the existence of Sasquatches. We can thus safely eliminate the hoax hypothesis as an explanation for the mystery of Sasquatch prints found in the woods of North America.

4

NATIVE AMERICAN HISTORY

W isconsin, in my opinion, is arguably the most beautiful region of North America (though perhaps my having been raised there has biased me somewhat). Additionally, there are few states outside of Wisconsin that I have traveled to. Nonetheless, there is an argument to be made about the beauty Wisconsin possesses. Southwest Wisconsin is home to rolling hills, which are at their peak beauty during the bloom of spring and the leaves begin to change during the fall. The rolling hills must be seen for their beauty to be truly appreciated. Traveling through the rolling hills, with the farmland and creeks running through the land, is truly indescribable. As you travel east or north from the rolling hills, the land begins to plateau, yet there are still many breathtaking sights to see. As a Milwaukee Brewers fan, once again, I am somewhat biased when I say that the American Family Field (formerly known as Miller Park) is a spectacular destination truly worth the price of admission. Other sights worth seeing in Milwaukee include the Historic Third Ward, Fiserv Forum (Bucks in six), Summerfest, and anything involving Lake Michigan.

For those who prefer the countryside to cities, then Milwaukee may not be the best place for you. Traveling north would be better, as long as you avoid Green Bay. Although Green Bay is the smallest city to have an NFL team, it is still quite large (especially for those of us who grew up in small towns). Making a trip to Lambeau Field is worth the drive itself. Moreover, Green Bay has some of the best freshwater fishing in the world. There are few places on Earth better for catching musky, walleye, or bass. If Green Bay and Milwaukee do not sound like the best place for you, you may instead prefer the small towns—with their ample camping grounds—of northern Wisconsin. As for northern Wisconsin, the woods stretch from the upper peninsula of Michigan into Minnesota. Most of this territory is sparsely populated.

Northern Wisconsin is comprised of many small rivers and lakes, which add to its beauty. Additionally, there are many different species of animals up north in comparison to southern Wisconsin due to the relatively low human population in the region. Among others, there are bears, wolves, and porcupines that can be seen more frequently than elsewhere in Wisconsin. Northern Wisconsin also has great fishing and hunting. Needless to say, Wisconsin has a little bit of everything, which can attract many people. Although Wisconsin is beautiful now, it was arguably even more so 500 years ago. The old-growth forests would have made an already immaculate land even more pristine. The animals that are plentiful now would have been even more so back then. The fishing and hunting would have had the potential to produce bigger game than today, even if the hunting process itself would have been more difficult due to the simpler equipment used.

Admittedly, while my statements about Wisconsin being the most beautiful state are biased, there is a lot of truth to what is written above. There are many states that are also incredibly beautiful, and each state offers visitors something unique. It is also true that all states would have been more naturally beautiful 500 years ago. When people journeyed from Asia to North America, they were venturing into uncharted territory. That venture had a much larger impact than what these people at the time could have possibly realized. They were stepping onto land that would eventually become Canada and the United States of America. The land would have been both immaculately beautiful and terrifyingly dangerous. The animals that lived there would not have had a reason to fear humans due to their lack of experience with them (until early humans started hunting these animals). Many animals traveled over the land bridge with these early humans, but there were still plenty of those that were native to North America and had never had contact with humans. That means that there were animals that would have viewed early humans as either a source of food or with no real interest (or fear) at all. Having to cope with the perils of the journey, as well as the dangerous animals, made the trip's success that much more astounding.

These early humans had many years to adapt to the local flora and fauna. We often overlook this as, today, we are quick to adapt to new situations with ease due to our ever-increasing technological advancements. Then, however, they would have had far greater difficulty adapting to these situations, which is why early humans should be given the credit that they deserve. Traveling to a new land filled with hostile terrain and wildlife and mastering survival to the best of their abilities is a feat that should not be taken for granted. Due to these survival techniques, these new natives would have had a masterful understanding of the animals around them. Indeed, they had to know which animal was friend or foe or pay the price. The Native American (and First Nation) tribes are not alone in this respect: natives of all lands tend to have a better understanding of how an animal lives with others in its environment than outsiders. Naturally, scientists who dedicate their lives to studying specific animals have an extraordinary understanding of them. However, they lack the expertise and know-how that a native of a region would have due to their close proximity to an animal.

Using the information gained from native populations tends to be scientists' preparatory stages when seeking to find and study an animal of a specific region. The native's knowledge becomes that much more valuable when the animal in question is highly elusive. Considering how much information we have gained from native populations from around the world about animals, scientists should be more open-minded to native claims about the existence of an animal. Native American and First Nation tribes say that there exists an animal yet to be classified by Western science. This animal—said to closely resemble humans—goes by many names, yet the two that do not appear in their language are likely the ones you are most familiar with: Bigfoot and Sasquatch. The disagreement between mainstream science and Native American lore is rather fascinating here. On the one hand, science's achievements and mastery technologically outstrip Native American societies. On the other hand, Native Americans have often been deferred to for their knowledge of a particular region and tend to have a far better understanding of how animals exist with the surrounding environment.

As has been (and will continue to be) mentioned in this book, suggesting that a large bipedal ape is currently living in North America is a bold claim to make. It should also be noted that North America's native populations have been making such a claim for centuries. This becomes even more interesting when we note that the descriptions of Sasquatches are shockingly similar from region to region among these tribes. Different tribes—which had precisely zero contact with one another—have described extremely consistent encounters. One fundamental of the scientific process is repeatability. As such, the fact that there is significant consistency among Native American stories about Sasquatches should not be overlooked.

Among the areas with stories of Sasquatch-like beings, the continent's northwest region should be recognized as being of the utmost importance. Due to its geographical location and its inaccessibility, this region would have been the last to have received information regarding the discovery of African apes in the 19th century. Accordingly, when stories of apes emerge from this region, we must seriously consider that a living ape is involved.

> The first published mention of the Columbia River carbines is by the pioneer paleontologist O.C. Marsh in

1877. In an address to the American Association for the Advancement of Science meeting in Nashville, he said, "Among many stone carvings which I saw there [Columbia River] were a number of heads, which so strongly resemble those of apes that the likeness at once suggests itself."[1]

All of the stone heads share similarities, including what appears to be a brow ridge. Moreover, the folds of skin near the brow ridge, which are seen in gorillas, are features also shared between these stone heads and other apes. The stone heads have details like those mentioned above, which happen to correspond almost perfectly with descriptions of Sasquatches reported from sightings.[2] When Roderick Sprague, to whom the above quote is attributed, showed these (centuries-old) stone heads to biologists, their response was of note:

> Roderick Sprague, an anthropologist at the University of Idaho, showed these heads to some biologists who positively identified them as representing high primates. When told where they were found, these biologists then pointed out how clearly they represented bighorn sheep.[3]

It is highly telling indeed that these biologists instantly changed their (previously confident) opinion based solely on where the heads originated. As we will discuss later in the book, there is an academic bias against the Sasquatch. These biologists most likely changed their interpretations out of fear of the implications.

> At the Maryhill Museum, where some of these heads are displayed, there is also a carved stone head from the same source that does represent a bighorn sheep, and it is obviously different. Whoever carved these heads had a good knowledge of what an ape's face

looked like. How they gained this knowledge remains to be seen.[4]

Any descendant of this tribe would be insulted at the insistence that the stone heads were all bighorn sheep. These natives were familiar with bighorn sheep, and to suggest that their carvings—which showed a clearly distinct animal—depicted a bighorn sheep would be an insult to their intelligence. They knew the animals in their area. Clearly, from their stone head carvings, they also knew the difference between an ape and a bighorn sheep.

An examination of another First Nations mask from the British Columbia area poses many questions as to how they acquired the knowledge they did as the mask represented "a mythical being found in the woods and called today a monkey."[5] We ought to remember that this region would have been the last in the West to be exposed to the discovery of the great apes in Africa.

> ... whether or not this mask is a portrait of a creature actually seen, it suggests to those who see it that it has some relevance to the Sasquatch, a zoologically unverified ape-like animal believed by both whites and Indians to inhabit forested regions of British Columbia.[6]

Confronted with these facts, the hoax hypothesis becomes even more inexplicable. One would have persuasively detailed how knowledge of the African apes made its way to this distant geographical location. Furthermore, this knowledge would have immediately resulted in ceremonial masks and stone head carvings. Moreover, it would have also had to integrate itself into native oral traditions. The alternative is that there exists an ape living in North America.

> One obvious explanation, and one supported by a number of people, especially those who have reported

seeing these monsters, is that these creatures really exist in the West.[7]

This would also explain why stories of Sasquatch-like beings are so popular among Canadian and American tribes. Ask yourself this, which hypothesis relies on more assumptions regarding why apes are represented in so many native traditions: the hoax hypothesis or the great ape hypothesis?

Although many of the tribes and areas we have focused on are from the Pacific Northwest, there is an eastern Canadian First Nation tribe that describes a creature eerily similar to the descriptions of western Canadian tribes:

> Those who claim to have seen the Wetikoo say that he is a terrible looking creature; his hair is long and matted. Living like a wild beast, ever exposed to the elements, never washing himself, he has a face which brings horror to those who see him... the terrible odour which is said to be most noticeable when he is near.[8]

The terrible odor mentioned here shares very strong parallels with the strong odors reported in modern-day Sasquatch encounters. Before we continue, we must first explain the difficulties in correctly categorizing Sasquatch sightings/traditions. Before the PGF, the use of the term "Bigfoot" was relegated to northern California. After the film's release, the name was used to describe what people had been seeing for centuries throughout North America. That marked the first time that there was an official name with which to categorize what people were, and still are, seeing. As such, we can expect that it would be rather difficult to categorize Native American traditions of these animals due to the variations in name. The information covered by most of these quotes comes from a relatively small tract of land. These beliefs are held by many Native American and First Nation tribes, not just from this area but from all over North America. Although many who have studied these tribes would have encountered stories of Sasquatch-like entities, they perhaps paid insufficient attention as they would have been unsure as to what these stories truly represented.

As unbelievable as a hitherto undiscovered large primate in the woods of North America sounds, is it any more improbable than the existence of the beaver (a large-toothed rodent who cuts down trees to block waterways), the electric eel (who produces more than enough electricity to kill a man), or of the platypus (an animal which defies conventional wisdom due to its unique body composition). It is worth mentioning that scientists of London's Royal Society insisted that the platypus was a hoax when it was first discovered. These are all real animals, is it really too much to think that the Sasquatch could also exist?[9] Part of the reason why there may be some hesitancy to accept these stories could be due to the absence of a common name for encounters with large apes fitting the description of Sasquatches before the popularization of the term "Bigfoot" in 1967:

> If there is a real animal, shouldn't there be better descriptions in the ethnographic literature. Not necessarily. Anthropologists do not consciously suppress information, but they sometimes do not know what to do with it. There are ethnographies of peoples whom I know to have traditions of sasquatch-like beings that make no mention of such traditions; I suspect that these omissions occur not because the writers had bever heard of traditions but because they did not know how to categorize them.[10]

Understanding the difficulty of categorizing Sasquatches in Native American and First Nation tribes helps explain why so many people have seen a similar creature but failed to recognize that the animal was the same as what others have been describing.

> Although there is not common name held for Sasquatch among Native American and First Nation

tribes one thing is certain, "But as things stand it seems we can only say that most if not all of the Coast Salish of this area seem to agree that there are large, man-like beings in the woods and mountains who differ from human beings in various ways."[11]

Indeed, this also helps explain why reports exploded after the PGF's release. For the first time in history, a common description of the phenomena of encountering a large bipedal ape had been provided. Due to the differences in names, many—if not all—anthropologists researching these stories may not understand that different names are being used to describe the same animal. "Since the names also vary, there might be a temptation to think that different species are being referred to."[12] Considering the similar descriptions and the way that "cross-genetic lexical borrowing," which uses a word derived from another language to describe a similar entity, we can see that similar words are used to describe an animal that fits the description of a Sasquatch. "As well, the cross-genetic occurrence of the forms which floss as man in words or man of the woods seems to have historical significance; viz., they are loan translations."[13] This highlights the need for a systematic study of the words and stories used to describe Sasquatch-like beings in order to determine whether there is validity to the theory that they all represent the same animal.

It should be considered significant that there are so many stories that describe similar entities in native folklore. So far, we have detailed stories mostly originating in Canada, but the next one comes from California, "the creature today called Bigfoot seems clearly to have been a figure of some concern in native northwestern California since aboriginal times." (152, Buckley) As some people claim that Sasquatches are merely mythical creatures, they tend to disregard evidence concerning their existence as no more than mythical stories. Some argue that, due to the fantastical nature of some of the stories, their veracity should be dismissed out of hand. However, those who make this argument fail to recognize that most, if not all, animals that are presented in oral traditions have some kind of mythical element to them. Let us consider the eagle as an example. Many oral traditions depict eagles as having certain mythical elements, yet we know that they conclusively exist. Living, at least in part, in the mythical aspect of traditional oral stories does not constitute evidence against one's existence. The stories of Sasquatch-like-beings are not considered hard evidence in the same way that footprint casts are. However, these encounters should still be treated as evidence.

> I am convinced that the Sasquatch exists, but whether it is all that it is cracked up to be is another matter altogether. There must be *something* in northwest America that needs explaining, and that something leaves manlike footprints. The evidence I have adduced in favour of the reality of the Sasquatch is not hard evidence; few physicists, biologists, or chemists would accept it, but nevertheless it is evidence and cannot be ignored.[14]

We should note that oral traditions are used as a reference for other animals that exist, meaning that we should consider them to be a fairly reliable indicator of an as yet unidentified species. Skeptics may argue that my last sentence was inaccurate due to the fact that there was no mention of the possibility that these beings are entirely mythical. While a case could be made that mythical creatures could exist in some form or realm (whether spiritual or mental), we must discount Sasquatches from this category as they leave behind physical traces of their existence.

> It straddles and incorporates boundaries that we consider absolute, that are fundamentally required by our system of rationality. To the extent that it is as it appears to be a being of the mind which leaves footprints in the earth-Sasquatch remains absolutely inexplicable, a genuine mystery. And so my suggested

reformulation of the Sasquatch encounter as a classic experience of the supernatural fails in the end, since our culture denies that the supernatural can manifest directly in the world, leaving material traces in the ground. Looking at a plaster cast of a Sasquatch footprint, I must confess to total bafflement.[15]

Focusing on one of the many stories from the tribes of the Coast Salish region, which details "a race of beings who live inland or on mountains, are twice the size of a man, with hairy hands, wide but deep-set eyes, black bodies."[16] Although skeptics may consider this description insignificant, we must remind them of the similarities between this description and those of modern-day Sasquatches. This type of evidence is considered anecdotal. However, when taken into consideration with everything discussed so far in this book, it becomes that much more important to the debate. Mythical beings do not leave footprints in the woods, nor are they filmed by cowboys in northern California. Besides, we should not dismiss native people as stupid. They have long lived with, and become accustomed to, the animals in the forests of North America. They know their stories, as well as the difference between reality and fiction.

> He seemed to view the supposed creature as a rather mundane beast. There seemed to be nothing special about the wild man except that he was a nuisance to farmers and a mild danger to hunters. He seemed to be too rare to be of any importance. When I tried to suggest that this wild man was comparable to the giant in the fables that Saygili had previously been relating to me, he became offended. He accused me of thinking him stupid and not able to tell a fairy tale from a real animal.[17]

These stories further the claim that any accounts of encounters with Sasquatch-like beings should only be considered as anecdotal evidence. However, I would instead claim that, combined with evidence from the PGF and the footprint casts, scientists have more than enough proof to present hypotheses of the stories and begin their investigations. We must keep in mind that, while these stories may seem mystical or fantastical, ghostly aberrations do not leave footprints.

We must now discuss the importance of understanding the difficulty of categorizing an animal that many claim does not exist. What should one term these oral accounts? More importantly, how does one go about categorizing them? There are many potential answers to these questions and therein lies the problem: there are many different names that apply to these animals, which means that there is no one single way to categorize them. Each person reading such stories can interpret them differently. Indeed, we can infer that these stories then may be categorized under various different areas of research. The difficulty here is that a potential animal exists—as evidenced by sightings, films/photographs, and footprints—yet the relevant information or proof may be missing (or miscategorized) due to the uncertainty from these native accounts. While our argument does not rely on these reports, it still would be useful to recategorize these stories in order to gain a comprehensive understanding of their potential implications.

Continuing our discussion of native people and their interactions with the animals in their environment, we must understand how the relationship between animals and humans before the industrial revolution. We know that most animals now are very skittish of people and tend to avoid contact. This would have been true to a certain extent among early native encounters with animals as well, except that these animals would have had less cause for fear. Guns were not introduced into the area until after European expansion into the Americas. That meant that most natives would have used spears or bows for hunting. Guns scare animals, largely due to the extremely loud sound that accompanies a bullet. Animals were also hunted less as natives did not have a way to store food, so they killed only what they could eat. Animals were hunted less often and with less fear-inducing materials. This means that, while animals may have been scared of humans, they were not as petrified to the same extent as today.

As soon as Europeans started spreading across North America and industrialization began, so too did the hunting of North America's big game. This drove many animals to the brink of—and in some cases into—extinction. As such, these animals learned to fear humans more so than what they would have needed to before. Knowing all of this presents the possibility that native people would have had longer interactions with animals. I use the word "possibility" here as the native people would not have wanted to have longer interactions with dangerous animals, such as bears or wolves. However, if the animals of the time were less fearful of humans, then the natives had the potential to have longer interactions with them. This could explain the abundance of Sasquatch stories from virtually all Native American and First Nation tribes—they lived in close contact with this creature long before Europeans arrived in North America.

Something that needs to be emphasized is that oral traditions are sometimes fantastical so as to better convey an easily told story. A story with painstaking (and often dull) accuracy is harder to remember than a partially accurate, fun, and exciting one. Think back to your time at school and compare a fun teacher to a boring one. You were no doubt more engaged with the fun teacher, making it more likely you remember what they taught you. The same is true of oral traditions passed down through the generations. The more fun/fantastical, the more likely one was to remember it well. Telling stories this way worked as long as they retained the central theme. The main message of the story remains the same, whereas the small intricate details are trimmed out for entertainment purposes. Stories are told to teach lessons or to pass down history through the generations.

" Native folklore often uses images of animals who are engaged in humanlike behavior as a vehicle for their cultural traditions and myths. The purposes of these stories can range from explaining origins to making little children behave... If one removes the obviously added human and supernatural aspects from the native mythology, some perfectly real animal descriptions are there to be observed. If one removes the same kinds of aspects from sasquatch tales, what remains is just what is so often reported by recent Euro-Americans.[18]

The fact that a story has fantastic elements does not eliminate it from representing a real phenomenon.

The Kwakiutl, another tribe located in British Columbia, also has depictions of apes in some of their ceremonial items. They have totem poles that depict the female Wildman as having "a prominent brow ridge, deep-set eyes, flaring nostrils and a wide grimace exposing large teeth."[19] One totem pole presents a female Wildman with noticeable breasts, long arms, and lips pushed out in a way to signify whistling.[20] The Tsimshian have ceremonial masks that are, like much of the other masks and stone heads in this chapter, shockingly close in anatomical detail with that of the African apes.[21] These two tribes are further examples of northwest North America's familiarity with apes, despite the seeming impossibility of this. Although it may seem highly improbable that these depictions are representations of a living ape in North America, this is far more likely than claiming that knowledge of African apes somehow made its way to these tribes and influenced them enough to include them in their ceremonial objects. If that truly is the case, then why do we not see other African animals represented in their ceremonial objects? Surely an elephant would have been more impressive, fantastical, and worthy of inclusion within stories and ceremonial items? The explanations for these apes in native tribal traditions are certainly interesting phenomena. Generating explanations outside of there being a great ape in North America becomes increasingly difficult when we combine the information in this chapter with that of the rest of the book. This is the type of evidence we would expect to see if there was a population of apes living in North America. As such, it should add some credibility to those who claim to encounter apes in North America in modern times.

Now that we have established that significant evidence exists, we will now turn to the scientific resistance to the topic of Sasquatches. Due to the nature of the scientific process, there is a natural resistance that must take place in order to determine the validity of a presented theory. The next chapter will be an expansive look at some theories that are widely accepted today as common knowledge but was heavily resisted upon their initial proposal. Understanding scientific resistance will equip us with the necessary knowledge for understanding the overarching thesis of this book.

5

HISTORY OF SCIENTIFIC RESISTANCE

We should be truly grateful for the technological and scientific advances which have allowed us to reach incredible heights. Yes, there are still troubling issues that need to be resolved, but every system that has existed and will exist will encounter large problems. Think of how truly fortunate we are to enjoy the medical advancements that we do. Looking back on how medicine used to be practiced is quite humbling. People used primitive tools and techniques to deal with ailments that can be solved as simply as by looking up the cure on one's phone. People in the past were often used as guinea pigs without sufficient methods to justify the madness. Most of the past testing was done without the ethical guidelines that govern testing on humans today. Modern medicine always seeks to advance its cumulative knowledge as efficiently as possible while also taking care not to endanger the lives or wellbeing of its contributors.

There are many issues that we do not have to deal with due to the successes and failures of the past. While working at a nursing home, a resident told me of their experiences with polio. Three other residents detailed what life was like growing up without heat, electricity, or running water. Those poor people would have to walk outside to the outhouse on those dreadfully cold Wisconsin winter nights. We are so advanced today that we are likely to mistake stores from the last century as being from the last millennium. We should thus be truly grateful that the poorest person living in the United States today is living in better conditions than those of people living 100 years ago.

Medicine is not the only field to have had many technological advancements. Baseball, among other pro sports, has much better protective gear and on-hand doctors who can help athletes recover more quickly and effectively from injuries. Cars today are so much safer than when they were first created. Farming practices are more efficient, cleaner, and environmentally friendly. Of course, some issues do still emerge as a result of the new techniques and technologies used. However, as a whole, virtually every aspect of life has dramatically improved over the last 100 years. Science is no different.

Science, much like everything listed above (and so much more), has had its fair share of growing pains. No institution has been or ever will be perfect. That is why we should be grateful, as the history of all of these fields is filled with countless failures. While these failures could have been enough to stop all of these advances in their tracks, they served only to spur innovation on. Indeed, failures routinely deter people from doing the things that they love. However, these fields were all furthered by people learning from the mistakes of the past and attempting to refrain from committing them again. The scientific process has been established so as to encourage mistakes as the optimal way for approaching the truth. This is why we see resistance in the scientific process throughout history.

While this last statement may be something of a generalization, it is a somewhat accurate representation of how the scientific process works. Ideally, scientists are supposed to report their theories, which are then attacked (for lack of a better word) by other scientists. Theories present in the scientific community are therefore those that have survived natural resistance. Somewhat analogous to natural selection, weaker theories die off due to their inability to survive the scrutiny of scientists. That is, by and large, how the scientific process operates, which we will now review.

For many centuries, people in the geocentric model of the universe, which put Earth at the center of the galaxy. This was not an unreasonable notion to hold due to the primitive astronomical knowledge and tools available at the time. Claudius Ptolemy hypothesized in the 2nd century that the Earth was at the center of the universe. Ptolemy's theory was generally accepted for many centuries. That theory stood until the 16th century. Nicolaus Copernicus published a paper in 1543 that challenged this belief and meant to build a new model of the universe. "Even as late as 1640," debates raged over the model of the universe. Many found it hard to accept a new model of the universe as the previous model had been so firmly established and adhered to. Gradually, the old model was replaced by the new.[1] It is important to note that what we learn from our mistakes helps us to significantly further our understanding of a subject. Science is no different in this aspect. Scientists use their mistakes or invalidated theories to formulate new or better ones altogether. We should not criticize Ptolemy for presenting a theory that was later revealed to be wrong. Instead, we should commend his scientific endeavors (conducted with the knowledge available to him) is proposing a new hypothesis. We should also note that the new heliocentric model of the universe faced fierce scientific resistance. However, as it was a strong theory, it was able to survive the relentless attacks it was subjected to.

Much like the heliocentric model of the universe, the theory of evolution has become an accepted part of our cumulative knowledge. However, this was certainly not always the case. Darwin's theory, to the surprise of no one, was highly controversial when first proposed. The theory was not readily accepted upon the release of Darwin's book, *On the Origin of Species*, and the man himself was criticized and vilified for having proposed such a theory.[2] The story becomes all the more interesting when we recount the fact that it took an enormous amount of debates among many of the best minds the scientific community had to offer to accept the theory. The theory threatened the traditional, Biblical interpretation that was the status quo. This is where the fun begins. Scientists tried to dismantle the theory. They used different methods to try to do so. And yet, not only did the theory withstand these attacks, but it even became all the stronger because of them. In fact, Einstein, the intellectual genius revered by scientists and laypersons alike, faced this same resistance as well. Einstein presented his theory of relativity to the world to similar (though less vitriolic) controversy in the scientific community.[3] Yes, even the great Einstein was not beyond scientific resistance.

As you continue reading this chapter, do bear in mind that the discoveries mentioned were unknown for the vast majority of human history. Although this may seem like an obvious statement, it is important to put yourself in the shoes of those who lived before the discovery to fully grasp the evidence that existed and the resistance encountered. For a modern example, look no further than COVID-19. None of us knew about the virus until late 2019/early 2020. This is an example of a phenomenon that existed that we were previously unaware of, and, once we learned of its existence, it changed our perception of the world. The discoveries mentioned here should be viewed in a similar light. We should also remember that the COVID-19 pandemic serves as an excellent example of the scientific process in real-time. Think back to how often you heard contradictory information. There were many medical experts who contradicted themselves with their use of masks. Dr. Fauci went back and forth on the usefulness or utility of masks many times. The reason for this back and forth is so often due to the nature of the scientific process. Theories are tested over and over again, from every possible angle, in order to determine their validity. While it seems that scientists may actually double back on what they said—which they may occasionally do—it must also be considered that the scientists are testing the previously tested theories with new information that they gathered. The lack of a concrete answer for some of these questions faced during the pandemic shows that science is a considerably time-consuming process.

Returning to our examples of resistance to ideas, we will look back to one of the greatest discoveries in all of history: Christopher Columbus's discovery of the Americas. Any American will undoubtedly remember the tune taught to us in school, "In 1492, Columbus sailed the ocean blue." While we are taught about Columbus for many years while in school, we do not truly comprehend the significance of his discovery. While it is true that the new world had already been discovered by the native populations living there, Columbus gets the credit for introducing the continents to the rest of the world. He is the one who struggled through resistance to be even allowed to make his amazing discovery. To better understand this moment, we must put ourselves in the shoes of those involved.

It would benefit us to correct a major misconception routinely taught in schools. Although there are those today who believe that the Earth is flat (albeit with possibly suspect motives), few people believed this in 1492. This goes against the notion we were taught in school that sailors were afraid to make the trip because of the possibility of falling off the world's edge. There are many reasons to discredit this all too common argument. First, looking at the moon cycling through the lunar phase is clearly indicative of a spherical object. Furthermore, modern cities are highly polluted and built up, thereby obscuring the night sky. The sky would not have been so obstructed half a millennium ago, meaning that these lunar phases would have been visible for most people. Second, one can clearly see the curvature of the night sky. The view under the stars gives us the impression that we are sitting under a dome. Third, the sun is round, why would people assume the Earth is flat while the sun is round? Moreover, they knew the moon was a sphere, so it follows that they inferred the sun to have the same shape.

But wait, you might say if Columbus and other sailors were not afraid of falling off the edge of the Earth, then why were they afraid to travel west toward the Americas? The answer is simple: because they did not know the actual distance to the next landmass, and thus whether they would survive the journey. The fear would have been rational because of the lackluster storage equipment for food and water. They did not know how much food they would need to sustain them through their journey, if it would last long enough for their next resupply, how far the next landmass was, or if they could return from wherever their journey would take them. Knowing all of this, it is all the more surprising that Columbus actually made the journey. Not only were the odds against him, but so were many people.

Columbus believed the Earth to be smaller than what it actually is. He believed that he had the ability to navigate from the West to the far East without having to travel down and around Africa. Columbus, for his part, had the courage to attempt the journey, but not the funds. The thought of discovering a new and faster trade route would seem to be an opportunity that any European country would jump at. However, finding the money for the expedition was not an easy task. After many failed attempts to gain the necessary money from Portugal, he decided to try his hand at another country: Spain. Failing with Portugal did not deter Columbus, who went to the Spanish crown and received the funding he needed for his expedition. The rest is history.

Although Columbus may not have faced resistance from the scientific community in the same sense as the other discoveries in this chapter, the resistance he did face is still worthy of our attention. I cite his case due to its being analogous to scientific resistance. He had an idea, which people initially disbelieved; he yielded results, leading to his acceptance. At first, the idea of two new continents did not fit into people's general understanding. Then, Columbus showed them direct evidence for the new world.

> We have direct evidence for a surprisingly small number of the beliefs we hold. For most of our beliefs (maybe almost all of them), we believe them largely because of the way they fit in with a large package of interconnecting beliefs. In other words, we believe what we do largely because of the way our beliefs fit into our worldview."[4]

Columbus' story also serves as an example of how one can be correct in the face of overwhelming disbelief from one's peers.

Continental drift was another theory that was initially dismissed due to the prevailing belief that the oceans and continents were fixed in their current positions.[5] We know now that this is not the case and that the continents move ever so slightly each year. Plate tectonics were not taught in school until approximately the 1970s. The original theory had the oceans and continents as stagnant, but this was eventually was superseded by the notion of plate tectonics. Interestingly, and pertinent to our cause, the original theory made many more assumptions than the plate tectonics theory, which replaced it. The theory that an asteroid wiped out the dinosaurs was hotly contested for many decades. The theory was met with extreme backlash and caused intense disagreement among scientists for many years. Now, the theory is widely accepted by the scientific community.[6] These theories, which are common knowledge today, were originally met with resistance from scientists. This resistance strengthened the theories and allowed for their mainstream acceptance due to their having been able to withstand intense scrutiny from contemporary scientists.

There are more examples of stories of initial rejection followed by scientific acceptance regarding the animal kingdom. When it comes to animals whose existence people disbelieved, the platypus is near the top of the list. Indeed, if you had never seen a platypus before and then had one described to you, you would be inclined to believe that such an animal could not exist. While Aboriginal Australians were fully aware of the existence of the platypus, it remained an unknown species to the international community for quite some time. Then, in the 19th century, a pelt was brought to London for examination. From what we are led to believe about the scientific community, we would think that a body, or a portion of a body, would be enough to validate the existence of a species. Interestingly enough, most scientists believed the pelt to have been stitched together from many different animals. Although it is now accepted as a living species, the platypus faced resistance to its discovery.[7]

Look no further than the great apes, and you will see that there was resistance to their discovery. Rumors of manlike monsters emerged from Africa. The locals had seen these monsters many times and knew that they were all too real. Interestingly, and amusingly, locals (as laypersons) tend to know of an animal's existence long before the scientific community does. The African great apes and platypuses are examples of this. As is the Okapi, which is believed to have been known by the Persians as early as 525 BC—yet not recognized by scientists until 1901.[8] We should note that this is part of what has been argued in the last chapter. Native populations have a better understanding of the animals in an area than widely regarded researchers. There are many more cases like these where natives knew of the existence of an animal, but scientists did not. Later, these natives were proven correct when scientists found the evidence they needed to validate the animal's existence. The African apes follow a similar line. The natives knew they were real. Stories emerged from these regions about these animals, but it was not until scientists ventured into these areas and conducted serious research that they were eventually "found."

Another theory that we should discuss is that of meteors falling from the sky. Chicken Little claimed that the sky was falling, which was, of course, incorrect. Today, we know that debris falling from the sky is likely attributable to meteors. Like all of the other examples in this chapter, the discovery of such an occurrence was far from straightforward:

> At that time, it was fashionable for savants to poke fun at the "absurd" belief that stones could fall from the air. After such a fall of stones at Julliac in France was witnessed by three hundred persons in 1790 and attested in a legal affidavit, the witnesses were ridiculed in the scientific press. An "obviously wrong fact... a phenomenon *physically* impossible," said one editor who felt nothing but pity for the witnesses. However, by 1803 the scientific men of the time had done a complete

turn around and decided that the falling stones were real after all.[9]

The importance of this discovery cannot be overlooked. The ridiculing of witnesses for seeing something that defied current scientific explanation is significant as:

> The effect on reporting is correspondingly negative. Few people enjoy being laughed at. The person who is willing to report an anomaly when several fraudulent reports have recently been exposed is hardy indeed. Many persons who would be willing to make a detailed report if they could find someone sympathetic to report to are discouraged by initial negative receptions created by this atmosphere. The fraudulent report is thus likely to constrict the reporting process.[10]

Why would (so-called) open-minded scientists ridicule someone? A large component of their job is to be open to all ideas and test the validity of anything they are presented with. Besides, if facts can be proven so easily, surely there is no need for ridicule to make one's point.

History shows us that ridiculing people can have negative repercussions and that scientists can, and oftentimes are, wrong about their perception of an event. Making mistakes or being incorrect is no bad thing as long as one learns from the experience. However, regarding the Sasquatch phenomenon, scientists refuse to learn from their mistakes and instead commit the same errors made countless times throughout history. The only difference is that scientists today have the ability to look back at past mistakes and ensure that they do not repeat them. We can look back and realize that some of the above theories should have been accepted long before they were.

> Scientists and historians can cite many cases of scientific and technological claims, hypotheses, and proposals that, viewed in retrospect, have apparently taken an unaccountably long time to be recognized, endorsed, or integrated into accepted knowledge and practice.[11]

As such, understanding all of this opens our eyes as to why we are where we are today with regards to Sasquatches. Then again, we also have to remember that scientists hold certain personal or professional beliefs that, when presented with a new theory, will prevent them from showing academic objectivity. Worse yet, suppression of the theory may occur as the scientist in question allows for their personal beliefs to obstruct the development of a new theory.[12] The ideal for a scientist is to be unbiased and open-minded. However, we are beginning to see that this may well not be the norm.

> The good scientist is seen as an unprejudiced man with an open mind who is ready to embrace any new idea supported by the facts. As the history of science shows, its practitioners do not appear to act according to that popular view.[13]

Bernard Barber, a sociologist, wrote about this subject in his paper titled "Resistance by Scientists to Scientific Discovery." He noted that we have a stereotypical image of scientists as being open-minded. Barber argues that the opposite is true. He states that the history of science shows us that scientists instead tend to be close-minded and unwilling to listen to new ideas.[14]

We think of the scientific community as a near-perfect entity that can do no wrong. However, we fail to consider that the scientific community is comprised of people and fallible and imperfect people at that (much like the rest of us). It should be noted that what is true of the parts does not necessarily have to be true for the whole. However, scientists have shown us that this is the case with the mistakes of the past that they have failed to learn from. However, while teams of scientists collaborating to overcome challenges does help avoid some mistakes, it does not guarantee perfection. We only have a limited understanding of the world and the universe. We can only process the information that we have through the limited window of our understanding. When we are presented with information that we do not understand, we are quick to dismiss it. However, we rarely stop and consider that we may be the ones who are wrong because of our limited understanding of how certain information works within our universe. "Science carries us toward an understanding of how the world is, rather than how we would wish it to be, its findings may not in all cases be immediately comprehensible or satisfying."[15] This chapter is filled with examples of how people of the past could not comprehend how a set of facts fit into the world, which in turn led to resistance to these ideas. The same is true of the book as a whole with regards to Sasquatches. There are many examples of information in this book that point to an almost certain level that Sasquatches exist. However, scientists are not able to comprehend this information, thereby frustrating their discovery.

James Lind found in his 18th-century experiments that citrus fruits had a special property that helped prevent scurvy. Lind conducted experiments to determine this and then published a book on his findings. However, the British navy ignored these findings. As you can imagine, their navy servicemen suffered because of this.[16] It was the officers who eventually persuaded the rank-and-file sailors to accept the consumption of limes, thus (for a time) making British sailors the healthiest in the world. Resistance is not exclusively for major discoveries. Although this discovery is far from minor, it did not have the same repercussions as that of natural selection. Minor and medium discoveries can be subject to resistance as well. Of course, this is perfectly natural as it neatly fits into our understanding of the scientific process.

It takes time for people to comprehend new information, which is why a "discovery is a process and must take time."[17] I acknowledge that resistance is natural and should, in fact, be considered beneficial as it eventually strengthens the theory itself. However, there comes a point when resistance becomes defiance. It is natural for scientists to resist a theory, but the theory of large bipedal hominids living today has been present (in its current form) for over 50 years. There is enough evidence through footprint casts and photographs to warrant investigation. Are we still in the natural resistance phase of discovery, or have we come upon a new phase?

For all major discoveries, there has been a transition between the natural resistance and acknowledgment of the scientific community of a phenomenon. However, we have reached a point where the natural resistance that usually benefits theories has become nothing more than a needless obstruction. An evolution has occurred in the way the scientific community analyzes potential theories. We would like to assume that scientists would be happy to listen to a theory. Sadly, this is increasingly not the case.

We have been taught, since elementary or middle school, that the scientific process is a near-perfect method used to cull weak theories. As such, we inferred that the scientists who are part of this process must, therefore, be on a similar level of perfection as the process itself. Said inference differs wildly in theory and in practice. In reality, nowadays, especially, scientists are much less likely to listen to theories they disagree with. The burden of proof now lies on me as I have made a claim that many would consider controversial. The next chapter will provide evidence with which to further validate my claim.

6

THE SASQUATCH PARADOX

Baseball is a truly amazing sport. Pitching and hitting are markedly different, but they both contribute to the beauty of the game. Pitchers are throwing the ball faster and with more spin than ever before. These increased speeds and spin rates mean that the balls are that much harder to hit. Hitting a fastball traveling at over 95 mph is extremely difficult. This is made even harder by having to be ready for an off-speed pitch meant to catch you by surprise. The pitcher, standing on the mound 60'6" away from home plate, throws a fastball quicker than the blink of an eye and an off-speed pitch that perfectly pairs with the fastball. Sit fastball and the hitter is out in front of the off-speed pitch, either hitting for weak contact or missing the pitch altogether. Sit off-speed and the hitter will have no chance to catch up to any fastballs thrown by the pitcher. Pitches have a lot of movement on them. There are many pitches that begin in the strike zone but travel away from it due to their spin. There are also pitches that start outside of the strike zone only to later enter it. It is no wonder why, before MLB cracked down on foreign substance use (used to grip the ball better, causing higher spin rates), hitting was down across the sport.

As remarkable as modern pitchers are, they may well be

surpassed by hitters. Hitting a baseball is arguably the single hardest thing to do in all of the sports. Hitting a baseball is not only highly challenging for the reasons explained above but also for many more. The bats used have a very small area, called the sweet spot, which produces the least amount of vibrations when making contact with the ball. That means that there is a tiny area with which a hitter can make solid contact with the ball. Round bat, round ball, hit square. On top of that, hitters have less than half a second to decide if they should even swing at all due to the type of ball they are pitched. Consequently, hitters regularly fail. The best hitters have an average of around .300. It should be noted that on-base plus slugging (OPS) is used as a more reliable indicator of success than batting average. However, batting averages are still important to consider. The best hitters usually have an average of around .300, which means that the best fail seven out of ten times. Remember that is the average for the best hitters; the league average hitters fail far more frequently.

What separates the better hitters from the weaker ones is their ability to brush off failure. The best hitters have a mindset that every out they make means they are one at-bat closer to a hot streak. The best hitters thus have a locked-in mindset that helps them fail less often. Hitters are similar in this sense to the hypotheses of scientists. Both must be tested against the best opposition in order to determine their success (or validity). The only way we know how good a hitter will be is by setting them against the best pitchers. The same can be said about scientific theories. The only way that the soundest theories are separated from the weakest is through the rigor of peer review. The experts in the field test a theory and determine its validity. A theory getting peer-reviewed is analogous to a batter stepping into the batter's box.

Imagine the following scenario: you are a rookie about to experience your first action in the big leagues. You realize you are living the dream held by kids everywhere as you walk out to the batter's box. Saying that you are nervous is an understatement, but you are more than ready to face big-league pitching. Welcome to the big leagues. As for your reward, you get the pleasure of facing the best pitcher in the league, who is standing only 60'6" away. He is the monster that lives in the nightmares of hitters around the league. Your adrenaline is flowing, as is anyone's who faces this pitcher. You are doubly nervous as it is your first time in a big-league batter's box. However scared you might be, you still step into the box. You do not let fear get in your way. You earned the right to be here and you want to see what you are capable of. Hitters who failed to have a successful career are more than grateful to know that they tried with everything they had. You may fail—indeed, most hitters do. You stand in the box. The odds are against you, but you want to see what you can do. As you prepare to hit, the pitcher does something that perplexes everyone: he refuses to throw the pitch to you. You are insulted. All that you have worked for has been for nothing. How do you know if you are good enough if the very test to measure this refuses to be run, thus refusing to honor the commitment it is supposed to adhere to?

The above scenario is an analogous example of the Sasquatch Paradox. The great ape hypothesis, with a plethora of evidence to suggest its validity, is routinely ignored. There is reason to believe that the hypothesis *would* survive the peer review process. Except, when the theory is walking up to bat, the scientific community refuses to pitch. They do everything they can to turn a blind eye to the theory. They do not seriously test it, believing instead that doing so would waste their time. If the great ape hypothesis is so weak, then why do scientists ignore it? This question is at the center of the Sasquatch paradox. Assuming that the theory is weak, would it not be easy to simply come up with a stronger theory? It would appear that scientists are unwilling to take the time to do so. This would be equivalent to a Cy Young caliber pitcher (the pitcher who is voted by the Baseball Writers of America Association as being the best in his respective league) refusing to throw to a rookie because they would consider the effort a waste of their time and ability. Although most rookies fade into obscurity, there are still those that light the baseball world aflame, and to do that do, they must first stand in the box and best big-league pitching.

The scientific discussion and testing of theories is another important aspect of the Sasquatch paradox. These discussions have never occurred. The (supposedly near-perfect) scientific process has instead failed to take the great ape hypothesis seriously. As you have read so far in this book, there is significant evidence for the existence of Sasquatches. One would assume that that would mean scientists would be willing to, at the very least, examine the evidence, yet this seems to be far from the case. "Few scientists regard the topic with any seriousness."[1] How can it be that so-called open-minded scientists have paid this topic such little attention?

The explanation of the Sasquatch paradox will allow you to understand the answer to this question. The Sasquatch paradox occurs when scientists refuse to examine any evidence. Furthermore, it occurs when institutions punish scientists who do consider the evidence. Throughout history, historians have tended to create certain narratives that have stuck in our minds. One of those is that scientists are unbiased and are willing to openly test anything in order to inch closer to the truth.

> The good scientist is seen as an unprejudiced man with an open mind who is ready to embrace any new idea supported by the facts. The history of science shows, however, that its practitioners do not appear to act according to that popular view."[2]

Carl Sagan said that "openness to new ideas, combined with the most rigorous, skeptical scrutiny of all ideas, sifts the wheat from the chaff."[3] Scientists cannot conduct this process if they fail to uphold scientific ideals.

David Daegling mentions something interesting in his book. Something that we should not overlook:

> Science as an institution had its mind made up regarding Bigfoot before the Patterson film... What was on the film was of no consequence to that conclusion.

The film had to be fake because there is no such thing as Bigfoot.[4]

We need to dissect this statement in every possible way. Daegling once again admits that "Scientific practice—let's be honest here—is all about making mistakes."[5] The importance of making a mistake is that one can learn from it and thus refine one's knowledge or processes. How many scientists in the past have described an idea as impossible, only for that impossibility to become a reality? This has happened so many times that scientists should be open to every idea, even if we currently have a greater cumulative knowledge now than we have ever done. Scientists claim to be open-minded, but they openly admit that they will ignore Sasquatch evidence. Imagine if I said that climate change cannot be real, therefore, it is not real. That would be enough to trigger these scientists into making an example out of me and my bad argument. Rightfully so, but these same scientists use the very same argument to dismiss Sasquatches.

I question why scientists are so afraid to discuss this topic. Here is the only logical way to look at the situation: we can assume that the argument for the existence of Sasquatches is extremely weak because, according to scientists, there is no way that Sasquatches can be real. Assuming this assertion is true, as it most certainly follows logically, scientists, as the (self-purported) proponents of the scientific process, would easily be able to refute my argument. You could argue that they do not want to waste their time arguing with people about a topic with an obvious answer. If that was the case, we would not see scientists arguing with members of the Flat Earth Society. Look no further than Neil deGrasse Tyson's video directed toward the rapper B.o.B. Tyson, a highly respected astrophysicist, took the time to refute a bad argument. Besides, if people who investigate Sasquatches are wrong, then expert scientists would be the perfect people to show us the error of our ways. That way, we can use our mistakes as lessons with which to improve in the future. Any scientist reading Daegling's words should be truly troubled. Of course, not at Daegling himself, for he only stated the truth, nothing more.

The problem that scientists are currently experiencing is that they are not letting the evidence take them to the conclusion. Instead, with Sasquatches, they already have already arrived at their conclusion and only seek out evidence to validate their preconceived conclusion. "The willingness to follow the data wherever they lead is balanced by the rigor to properly collect, analyze, and report those data, and what they appear to indicate."[6] This is a true representation of the scientific process as this serves to eliminate confirmation bias. Everyone, scientists included, is biased. The scientific process is designed to remove this bias as far as is possible, though this can only be done when scientists follow the process. The situation with the topic of Sasquatches occurs when scientists fail to adhere to this process. Scientists ignore the topic, which prevents them from seeing the importance of the evidence that currently exists. All the more reason to follow the scientific process so as to better understand such contradictions.

We know that science ignores Sasquatches for many reasons, one of which is out of embarrassment of being wrong, "if there were anything to it, why were the 'experts' so late at recognizing it."[7] Better to pretend that you (scientists) did not make a mistake than acknowledge that a mistake could have occurred. Better to pretend than admit that you do not uphold the ideals you claim to endorse. Better to pretend something is fake than, as an expert, risk being wrong when many non-experts are right. When one claims that the Earth is flat, scientists are more than happy to jump at the opportunity to prove these individuals wrong. They will make videos debunking bad flat Earth theories. These videos, which can be found on YouTube, are often considered quite comical. Thus, it is clear that scientists of reputable standing will go out of their way to debunk theories of little merit. Scientists do this due to the ease of doing so while simultaneously educating the public. Why, then, do these scientists ignore Sasquatches? If it were so easy to debunk their existence, as it is with the flat Earth theory, then why ignore the topic? Surely, there is more evidence for the existence of Sasquatches than for the flatness of our planet. As such, we would expect it to be well within reason for scientists to challenge this theory. Instead, they simply ignore it.

Your first instinct might be to argue that Tyson himself has commented on Sasquatches. While this is absolutely true, we need to dissect his comments in order to continue our understanding of the Sasquatch paradox. With the enormous advances in communication technology, people nowadays frequently express their opinions on everything. This means that people inevitably express their opinions on subjects they may lack a fundamental understanding of. Look no further than Tyson's comments on Sasquatches. Tyson has made many comments on Sasquatches, both in one of his books and on Twitter. Before we discuss his comments, we should note the sudden appearance of several warning signs. Tyson commenting on Sasquatches should be concerning as he is looking in the wrong direction. Last I checked, there are no reports of Sasquatches in space, only from the wooded areas of North America. To where does Tyson devote most of his time: up in the sky or in the woods?

Tyson is a remarkable astrophysicist whose enthusiasm for his topic is infectious, thereby making him a truly great science communicator. Additionally, he helps simplify an enormously complex subject for the benefit of the layperson through his talks. We are not here to discuss the contributions that he has made to the field of astrophysics. Indeed, that topic is well out of my area of expertise. On the other hand, I am sufficiently informed on the topic of Sasquatches to discuss it in detail. The best way to describe Tyson and his Sasquatch comments can be found on his Twitter page. "A pernicious source of bad decisions in our lives... Knowing just enough about a topic to think you're right, but not enough to know you're wrong."[8] Although Tyson may not be making bad decisions with the information that he spreads about Sasquatches, he definitely hit the nail on the head with the second part of his tweet. Tyson knows just enough about Sasquatch to think that he is right, but not enough to know that he is wrong.

How do we know that he is wrong? Well, Tyson has stated that the "likelihood that a large (land) animal has gone unnoticed in modern times is near zero."[9] Obviously, the implicit meaning of this quote is sound as we believe ourselves to be aware of most of the (large) animals that exist. However, his error lies in what he is inferring. His inference is that Sasquatches are not real because we have not found one yet. It does not take an astrophysicist to determine that is the inference being made. As I stated already, Tyson is looking in the wrong direction. After reading his quote, many questions spring to mind, such as how informed is he regarding the search for elusive animals, has he studied the anatomy of Sasquatch footprints, has he conducted a systematic review of the photos of potential Sasquatches and has he reviewed the history of Wildmen/Sasquatch sightings throughout history? Even if he answered yes to all of these questions, did he review the information with an open mind, or had he already determined that Sasquatches cannot be real?

Something that I want to emphasize here is that I did not always believe in Sasquatches. When I first began my research, I was very skeptical about their existence. Indeed, I would have defined myself as an unbeliever. That is why I was shocked when I began my research. Specifically, Dr. Meldrum's book, *Sasquatch: Legend Meets Science*, convinced me that the reports of Sasquatches were authentic. I did not come to the topic already believing that Sasquatches were real—indeed, quite the opposite. I approached the subject with a skeptical lens and formulated my opinion after carefully and fairly reviewing the evidence. That is how science is supposed to work. And no, I am not a perfect scientist. In fact, I am what you would call an amateur scientist. Scientists have much more experience working with the scientific process and a greater understanding of science. I happily concede that they are my superiors in these regards, as I lack their experience and knowledge. However, there is one subject in which I better uphold the ideal that scientists must adhere to. Before you dismiss this statement, allow me to give you an analogous case. Professional sports are truly amazing in every sense of the word. Modern professional athletes are at the top 1% of the top 1% in the history of human athleticism. Furthermore, they have spent years honing their knowledge and expertise. However, there are some sports in which less-known players have better fundamentals. Look no further than college basketball. In the NBA, players play in a system that allows their athleticism to shine. College players cannot do the same as they are still growing into their bodies, which means that they must rely on the fundamentals of the game rather than pure athletic talent. When it comes to the fundamentals, there are many college players who are much more sound than their NBA counterparts. This is not to say that they are better than NBA players, of course, only that college players rely more heavily on the fundamentals. Due to my lack of experience in scientific investigation, I must rely more on the fundamentals of the scientific process in order to compete with the experts at the top of the scientific field.

To return to Tyson, we must ask ourselves, is Tyson truly knowledgeable of the subject of Sasquatches, or is he using his well-known name to make a point outside of his specialist field? We know the answer to this question. Dale Carnegie would call this an "exploitation of his name but not his forte."[10] Dr. Bindernagel describes Tyson's comments as an "Uninformed but authoritative scientist affirming the sasquatch as a cultural phenomenon."[11] Tyson's comments were made in response to an email he received from someone asking for his opinion on Sasquatches. The person then responded to Tyson's email, thus providing us with another quote to discuss. Tyson stated that if the person believes Sasquatch is real, he should "mount an expedition to find them."[12] This seems like a reasonable response, except it fails to address one of the pillars of the Sasquatch paradox that is evident from this statement. Scientists tell the world that science begins when a body is found—despite the fact that science never begins with a conclusion. This means that scientists are openly acknowledging their refusal to research Sasquatches. "Absence of evidence is not always evidence of absence."[13] The fact that a body has not been found is not sufficient for saying that a body does not exist. Why do scientists accept this as enough evidence to ignore Sasquatches? Returning to Tyson, he told an individual (we can safely assume) without scientific credentials to go out into the field and collect evidence. Scientists openly ignore the issue at hand, then tell amateur researchers to go and find evidence, only for these same amateurs to be dismissed out of hand due to their lack of credentials. This is a circular argument from scientists. Scientists use this lack of credentials to attack Sasquatch researchers and delegitimize any evidence that they collect while at the same time telling these people to gather evidence. Evidence should absolutely be attacked in order to determine its validity. However, attacking amateurs for their lack of credibility is paradoxical as these researchers are literally following the instructions of such celebrated scientists as Tyson. What is the solution to this paradox? Simple, scientists must conduct the research with an open mind.

Tyson also states in his first email that Sasquatches have gone unnoticed in modern times, and in his second that there is a lack of evidence. How does he know this? First, the BFRO has over 60,000 reported encounters. Hardly unnoticed. Of course, some of these encounters may not be genuine, but should we consider the accounts of Native American and First Nation tribes as unnoticed? In *A Quest for the Truth* (starting with the last paragraph on page 84), I claim that more Sasquatch encounters occur than are reported because people are afraid of ridicule. In fact, after publishing the book, someone approached me about how their ex-husband had had an encounter but was too afraid to talk about it. This is only one case, but I assure you that there are many others. Naturally, some of these 60,000 encounters will be hoaxes or misidentifications, but usually, that constitutes a small portion of reported sightings. Second, how does Tyson know there is a lack of evidence? Were he to study the topic from reputable sources, he would see that the opposite is true: there is a plethora of evidence. This was a great surprise for me when I began my research. At first, I believed that the only evidence was the PGF. However, I soon found that there was a surprisingly large amount of evidence for the existence of Sasquatches. I learned this only from diving into the research. Has Tyson done the same? If not, then perhaps he should not comment on the topic. Alternatively, if he must provide his opinion, he should acknowledge that he has not conducted extensive research on the topic. As Dr. Bindernagel stated, "no one can be convinced by proof one does not understand."[14]

This all sounds well and good, but how does it relate to the Sasquatch paradox that I claim exists? It is one thing to claim that a nine-foot ape lives in the woods of North America, but quite another to suggest that the scientific community is actively preventing its discovery. While bearing all of the above in mind, we will now turn our attention to scientists who research Sasquatches. In theory, these scientists should be commended for upholding the scientific ideal of free and unbiased inquiry. However, the truth is sadly different. Tyson can argue against Sasquatches, as is his right. However, doing so shows his (and many other scientists') hypocritical nature in commenting on a subject they lack an understanding of. This is slightly comical as Tyson would be the first to criticize anyone for spreading faulty information about astrophysics. Tyson really needs to remember one of his tweets: "The good thing about science is that it's true, whether or not you believe in it."[15] The existence of Sasquatches is true, regardless of Tyson's beliefs.

David Daegling admits that science openly and vehemently refuses to examine the evidence. Not only that, but Daegling mentioned how scientists routinely attack those within the community with less significant or impressive scientific credentials. John Napier was able to discuss Sasquatches openly only because he had the necessary credentials and a history of scientific excellence. He could do this without fear of losing his credibility.[16] Or could he? Napier is very skeptical in his book, almost to a fault. However, he expressed genuine interest in the subject in his private life.[17] It is telling that a highly respected scientist such as Napier had to hide his interest in Sasquatch out of fear for his reputation.

Napier was the Visiting Professor of Primate Biology at Birkbeck College, University of London at the time that he wrote this book on Sasquatches. He had significant scientific credibility. It is not insignificant that he felt the need to suppress his true opinions out of fear for his standing in the scientific community. (Author's note: several of Napier's quotes are used in Chapter 3. When reading his work, it is clear that he is overly skeptical about protecting his credibility while at the same time inferring the likelihood of the existence of Sasquatches.) This is the same community we are led to believe is open-minded, questions everything, and is willing and able to make mistakes so as to learn from them for the good of the discipline. Not only did Napier have to hide his true opinions, but scientists refuse to investigate Sasquatch "because to be associated with Bigfoot is tantamount to academic suicide."[18] Why is this the case? This question is one of the central themes of this book and a pillar of the Sasquatch paradox. Surely, if anyone had the credibility to discuss Sasquatches without fear of retribution, it was Napier. However, even he was unwilling to risk his reputation as he knew that convincing his community would have been a losing fight.

I believe that you should be, and possibly are, asking for more proof. You may accept the significance of Daegling's quote and the chapter as a whole, but this information, in and of itself, is not enough to fully persuade you. You would be quite correct in thinking so. This information should not be enough to fully persuade you. However, it should be enough to pique your curiosity about the validity of my claims. This means that the burden of proof now rests upon me to present you with a sufficiently convincing argument. Before we begin analyzing specific examples, let us first consider a quote from Dr. Bindernagel which mirrors Daegling: "Scientists who publicly express an interest in the sasquatch phenomenon risk doing serious damage to their reputations, and the institutions that employ them may frown upon even indirect associations with the subject."[19] Two different scientists who have looked into the phenomena have both reached similar conclusions: one cannot investigate the topic without receiving scorn or professional obstructions from the scientific community. The scientists who are interested in researching Sasquatches are too afraid to voice their opinions.[20] These scientists are not necessarily believers, simply those who feel that the amount of evidence warrants an investigation. "People silence themselves not because they are wrong but because they do not want to face the disapproval that, they think, would follow from expressing the view they believe to be correct."[21] These scientists are thus being prevented from fulfilling their scientific duties out of fear and intimidation.

Drs. Krantz and Meldrum will surely tell you the exact same thing. Not only was Dr. Krantz's tenure delayed by a year, but later "when my promotion to full professor was denied, the only reason the dean could come up with was that my work was not favorably received in all quarters."[22] It is certain that his promotion was denied due to his interest in Sasquatches. Krantz states that if the fact that his work was not favorably received by everyone, then "By this criterion, Charles Darwin and Albert Einstein could not have possibly gotten this promotion at my university."[23] Krantz also details the money that he lost. He says that he had spent approximately $100,000 on his Sasquatch investigations and that he lost, in his estimation, close to (if not more than) that same amount from being denied promotion.[24]

Napier, a public skeptic, would also support the claim of a fearful atmosphere surrounding the Sasquatch investigation. Napier called out his fellow scientists, who ignored the Sasquatch topic. While Napier himself was critical of the evidence, he was at least willing to listen to and examine it. Napier admits that the scientific community does not hold itself to its own standards.[25] Being skeptical is essential to the scientific process. However,

> the question is not whether or not to be skeptical. It is rather: Does being skeptical absolve relevant scientists from examining the evidence before discounting it and, in some cases, discrediting it in print?[26]

It should certainly be noted that any scientist who seriously looks at the evidence believes that an investigation is warranted. We need to look no further than Drs. Meldrum and Krantz, and all the fingerprint experts mentioned above. Both anthropologists damaged their careers by publicly endorsing Sasquatch research. What would possibly cause an individual to intentionally risk their own career? There clearly must have been enough evidence for both scientists to risk their reputations and careers. The counter-argument here would be to say that the two scientists simply wanted attention. Indeed, Dale Carnegie says that everyone wishes to feel important.[27] Is Dr. Meldrum's (and was Dr. Krantz's) interest in the subject just an act to gain attention and a sense of importance? This counter is deeply flawed. First, why would Dr. Krantz spend so much money on the subject out of his own pocket? Surely, someone wanting attention and a feeling of importance could have done so without such a massive financial investment. You may interject and ask how we know that Krantz invested so heavily into his investigations. That we cannot say for certain; however, it is a reasonable estimation seeing as Krantz includes photos in his book of the mini helicopter he bought to help him in his search.[28] Second, the fingerprint experts say that the footprints are legitimate. Are we supposed to believe that all of these experts are so interested in this feeling of importance that they are all willing to lie? Obviously not, because most of them did not pursue the matter any further. Third, what would have driven these two anthropologists to write books and articles on the subject? Writing books takes considerable time and effort. These two anthropologists' books are comprehensive, extraordinarily well-written, and are considered two of the finest books on the subject. It just does not follow that they would exert so much effort only to feel a fleeting sense of importance.

There is a simple reason why the scientific process results in resistance and delays discoveries: scientists must first report their theories and then subsequently defend them from academic attack. These attacks reveal the weakness with the theory that must be rectified in order to bolster its validity. Indeed, it is a fact that scientists are supposed to make mistakes and then learn from them. However, when it comes to the topic of Sasquatches, mistakes are not allowed. Any mention of the topic will result in the destruction of one's career and reputation.

We have reached a point where the natural resistance that used to benefit theories has transformed into something deeply detrimental. We have detailed in the last chapter the history of natural resistance to scientific discoveries. You might think that we are currently in that resistance phase. However, a stark distinction will help us understand why it is, in fact, defiance as opposed to resistance. This distinction comes from the fact that the topic of Sasquatches has not been debated within the scientific community (as is the case with other discoveries).

The Sasquatch paradox occurs when scientists completely reject the idea without seriously testing the possibility of its authenticity. Many theories throughout history developed over considerable periods of time while being tested by scientists. Furthermore, these same scientists tell laypersons—who lack both experience and credibility in the scientific community—to conduct research themselves. Are we honestly expected to believe that scientists will listen to these people if evidence is found? As we have detailed, the PGF is a tremendous piece of evidence. What happened when Patterson presented it to the scientific community for review? His character was attacked, and the film was dismissed as a hoax. Indeed, most scientists outright ignored the film. These are the same scientists who claim to be objective and open-minded. I question why most scientists, both then and today, chose not to investigate the film. If the film was as weak as claimed, disproving it entirely would have been fairly straightforward. However, we know instead of how truly challenging it is to find evidence with which to delegitimize the film.

Think hard on this question? If the scientific community is so open-minded to any idea, why were Meldrum and Krantz punished for their research? The scientific community should have been supportive of their research. Indeed, they were simply testing the strength of the great ape hypothesis—an action that stands at the heart of the scientific process. It is a way to cull the weak from the strong. Perhaps you will argue that the scientists of today are unaware of the evidence, which is why they shun those who talk about

Sasquatches. In that case, it would be of even greater importance for them to examine the evidence in order to understand its validity.

> And just because a phenomenon cannot be reconciled with what we now know, we need not shut our eyes to it. On the contrary, it is the duty of the scientists to try to devise experiments designed to probe its truth or falsity.[29]

In short, scientists believe Sasquatches cannot exist in our world, so they do not bother themselves with examining the evidence and instead shut down any conversation about the subject. However, they fail to accept the possibility that they may be wrong or their obligation to determine which of these two possibilities is incorrect.

Part of the problem is that scientists are too skeptical when it comes to Sasquatches. Granted, perhaps amateur researchers are not skeptical enough, so it may sound slightly unfair to say that scientists are too skeptical. Scientists are not supposed to be believers, nor are they supposed to be rigid skeptics. They are supposed to occupy the middle ground, allowing them to be open-minded while simultaneously being skeptical enough to properly conduct experiments. Skepticism causes some people (scientists included) to be so rigid in their belief systems that they close their minds to any new information. They already know what they know, and they do not want anything to jeopardize this knowledge.[30] Due to this, scientists are "hesitant to departure from the typical" theories presented as "scientists have accepted a self-imposed limitation on the hypotheses they are willing to consider."[31]

As mentioned above, the asteroid (or comet) that killed the dinosaurs was a theory that faced backlash and caused significant debate. Our need to focus on the latter as a heated academic debate is why the theory took its rightful place among accepted scientific discoveries. Natural resistance comes to a head when scientists debate an issue on which they disagree. The most convincing argument will naturally win the debate. This can, in turn, cause scientific perception to either change to a new theory or remain fixed on the current one. The important thing to note is that the debates actually occurred with the theories mentioned in the previous chapter. The reason that natural resistance has morphed into an artificial defiance regarding the Sasquatch question is that scientists refuse to conduct these debates. Indeed, they even refuse to discuss the topic with interested parties. The debates that helped shape some of today's best theories are not available for the topic of Sasquatches.

The debates necessary for validating a theory are simply are not being held for the great ape hypothesis. This is a troubling issue. While it is true that scientists nowadays have a larger cumulative knowledge than in the past, and we live in an advanced technological age, neither of these facts should allow scientists to ignore the issue. Scientists so firmly hold the belief that Sasquatches do not exist that they never for a moment consider the alternative.

> Still, another phenomena that gets us in trouble, I think comes from focusing too strongly on one particular channel or one particular idea. We make strong assumptions and get frozen into them. It's not only the fixed assumptions that we make; it's that we just have a habit of thought going down a particular path. And if that is successful and popular, and everybody's doing it, then we ignore another channel leading off somewhere perhaps more interesting.[32]

You cannot find a needle in a haystack without looking, and hoping to chance upon it would be utterly foolish. Scientists can best be thought of as individuals searching for the needle with a magnet. Granted, the needle would still be difficult to find, but the magnet will make all the difference in the right hands. However, having amateurs look for this needle without a magnet makes it painfully clear why the needle has yet to be found. Know that we have caught glimpses of the needle, even if scientists pretend that it does not exist. Having read up to this point of the book, we should now be aware that scientists' belief in the nonexistence of the needle is not as strong a position as we may have once believed. To use a movie reference, the Matrix existed for those who were plugged into it, regardless of whether they were aware of it or not.

There is another issue that must be addressed. Scientists have an unusual aversion to being compared with apes. Most animals are considered beautiful due to the important part they play in their environment. Apes, however, tend not to receive this same kind of love. Many scientists look down upon apes, possibly due to the similarities they share with humans, and as such feel as though apes are ugly or stupid.[33] They continue this by arguing that apes are not as smart as their human cousins. Indeed, Dr. Bindernagel argues that some fear the possibility of a bipedal ape as walking on two legs is often considered a separator between humans and apes.[34]

Unlike most animals, apes are oftentimes defined as being inferior to humans, possibly due to how we tend to hold them to our standards. In 1971, Friedrun Ankel-Simons argued for a classification to separate humans from primates. "Ankel–Simons separated humans from their embarrassingly close relationship with apes by establishing the order 'Biamana' (two-handed) for humans, and the order 'Quadrumana' (four-handed) for all other primates."[35] This quote shows that some in the scientific community (in 1971 and possibly today) are uncomfortable being compared to primates. "The existence of a habitually bipedal primate other than humans may be an unacceptable concept for many of us."[36] Dr. Bindernagel argues that many scientists may be afraid to acknowledge another bipedal ape out of fear of being compared to our "embarrassingly close" relatives. As I have stated before, blatantly dismissing Sasquatches due to preconceived notions (or fear) is a discredit to the scientific process.

Psychologically speaking, people do not want to feel wrong as it is an awkward feeling that forces us to swallow our pride and admit our own ignorance. The scientific community, being composed of people, shares this distaste for being in the wrong. Besides, they are supposed to be experts. We look up to experts as if they have all the answers.

No one has all the answers. Perhaps it is due to the changes in our society stemming from technological advances, but we are becoming worryingly arrogant and close-minded to new ideas. We also acquire information from disreputable sources and sometimes accept this information as absolute truth. You should not accept something as true just because you read it on the internet or someone close to you told you. Instead, you should listen to their argument and determine its validity. We are too quick to accept information before testing its strength.

Once people have an idea, they tend to cling onto it while fighting to be right. Although these people may not hold their beliefs for the right reasons, they are certainly willing to fight to the death to protect them. People would rather fight and argue than admit that they may be wrong. Think of the last time you admitted that you were wrong. Did you make a bad investment, give bad advice, or tell a lie? We have all done something wrong in our time. However, we do not all admit our mistakes. Look no further than politics. When a politician makes a mistake, they either come up with excuses, blame the opposition, or perform a set of linguistic gymnastics rather than frankly admit to their error.

Expanding upon this political theme, think back to the last time you had a conversation with someone who held different political beliefs. You likely heard what they had to say, but you did not listen. You did not listen because the person you talked with did not know as much about politics as you. You did not listen to any of their facts or analyses, nor did you ask them why they hold the beliefs they do. The conversation was likely an unproductive one. However, the other person is not to blame. You are because you did not take the opportunity to listen to them. Jordan Peterson, in his book *12 Rules for Life: An Antidote to Chaos*, lists Rule Number 9 as "Assume that the person you are listening to might know something that you don't." The reason that Peterson lists this specific rule is that many of us are content with what we know and are sometimes unwilling to listen to others.[37] We limit ourselves by thinking that we know everything, which may prevent us from opening our minds to a new, correct idea.

The same is true of the modern scientific community. They believe that they are right and are unwilling to listen to those who present contradictory information.

Sasquatches may initially be hard to accept. Bipedal apes living in North America? It is a strong claim to make, but so were so many others that have eventually been proven correct. Meteors, evolution, the theory of relativity, etc., all were ideas that contradicted what people knew at the time of their discovery.

> Is there an unknown species of animal that is very heavy, has human-like feet and walks erect? The very idea is ridiculous. Is there, then, a person or organization that has been using specialized equipment to make giant footprints over an area of hundreds of thousands of square miles, for the best part of a century, without being directed? That, too, is ridiculous. The only comfortable explanation is that the tracks don't really occur at all, but the plain fact is they do.[38]

Although the great ape hypothesis may seem far-fetched, the counterclaims made by skeptics are often more so. "Science... frequently contradicts the knowledge of common sense and direct experience." The consensus in the scientific community is that Sasquatch is not real. The evidence contradicts this.[39] After considering all of the information covered in this book so far, we know that the idea of Sasquatches living in North America is not far-fetched. In fact, the only reason scientists have not realized this is due to the fact that "their assumptions prevent them from considering what might otherwise seem to be an obvious possibility."[40]

The question we now have to ask is one with significant possible implications: is scientific artificial scientific defiance only occurring to the topic of Sasquatches? If yes, this would be highly troubling as it would indicate that the scientific community is not living up to its own ideals. However, if no, the answer is even more worrying. There has been insufficient research conducted on this particular issue for me to make any statements other than this is something that must be addressed. Hopefully, artificial defiance only occurs with the existence of Sasquatches. That way, we can learn from this mistake in order to improve the scientific process.

The defiance we see with Sasquatches notably occurred with the theory of evolution. In his article, "The Prematurity of Darwin's Theory of Natural Selection," Michael Ruse notes that:

> success at this level depends not only on the science within which a new idea is introduced but also on the constraints and implications of the state of the other impinging sciences. Until the physicists had made their moves on the age of the earth, natural selection simply was condemned to remain under a cloud.[41]

Ruse continues this argument:

> There were many other factors surrounding natural selection, both in its birth and in its subsequent development. Some of these were conceptual, like the extent to which adaptation and function were considered crucial questions for an evolutionist to address and answer... Some of these factors were more social and cultural, like the personalities of the players involved and the status of the science at the particular moment a new idea is introduced. All these things had their part to play, not only in the success that Darwin had with natural selection but also in the success that Darwin did not have with natural selection. I would not presume to generalize from this one case to all other instances of scientific discovery-even to only those that posterity judges premature-but I would be surprised if the tale of natural selection were unique.[42]

Ruse is simply stating that the evidence was abundantly clear after physicists made the age of the world known, that Darwin's theory was correct.

> Darwin brought beneath the hypothesis of evolution to explain different phenomena and the puzzling questions within these subsidiary areas of biological inquiry: behavior, paleontology, biogeography, systematics, anatomy, embryology, and more. He used the idea of evolution to explain different phenomena and the puzzling questions within these subsidiary areas, as when he explained the distributions of reptiles and birds on the Galapagos Archipelago as a product of migration from [the] South American mainland and subsequent divergence as the animals moved from island to island. Then, conversely, Darwin used his explanatory success in these various areas as collective confirmation of the veracity of the fact of evolution. How could a false claim explain so much?[43]

The theory was so hard for the religious and scientific communities to accept because it challenged the very foundations of their belief systems. That caused the theory to face defiance much in the same way that the great ape hypothesis faces defiance today. How could a false claim explain so much? How can the great ape hypothesis, if false, explain so much, whereas the hoax hypothesis, if correct, explains very little?

Scientists will defend themselves by relegating Sasquatches to the realm of pseudoscience. We will assess the validity of this. Carl Sagan defines science as:

> Pseudoscience differs from erroneous science. Science thrives on errors, cutting them away one by one. False conclusions are drawn all the time, but they are drawn tentatively... Science gropes and staggers toward improved understanding.[44]

Whereas he defines pseudoscience as:

> Pseudoscience is just the opposite. Hypotheses are often framed precisely, so they are invulnerable to any experiment that offers a prospect of disproof, so even in principle, they cannot be invalidated. Practitioners are defensive and wary. Skeptical scrutiny is opposed.[45]

Using Sagan's definition, we can see that Sasquatches do not fit within pseudoscience. Granted, there are those in the Sasquatch community that practice pseudoscience. However, when following Sagan's above explanation, we find something very interesting. The scientific community, as opposed to "believers," is the group that truly practices pseudoscience. Their hypothesis—Sasquatches cannot exist; therefore, they do not exist—has been framed as infallible. Scientists are defensive of the topic due to the risks to the careers of those who would discuss it. Skeptical scrutiny may not be opposed in this sense. However, as any discussion is prevented, it could be argued that all of Sagan's pseudoscientific criteria Sagan are met by scientists arguing against the existence of Sasquatches.

There are scientists who have delved deeper into the Sasquatch question only to hypothesize that hoaxers are the only suitable explanation. Although this hypothesis will be weakened in the next chapter, we should note that these scientists are not practicing pseudoscience. They are, however, the exception rather than the rule. The majority of mainstream scientists close their minds to anything Sasquatch-related. In so doing, they are themselves practicing pseudoscience, and yet they are quick to claim that believers are the pseudoscientists. As qualified scientists in the field, one would expect better from them. They claim to stand for the scientific ideal, but they fail to meet such a mark.

Ilhana Löwy explain the modern-day scientist so that we can understand why their beliefs are lacking in certain areas.

> The great majority of scientists, Kuhn explains, are not busy contesting accepted knowledge or falsifying major claims but instead repeat with relatively small variants-the work of their predecessors. Moreover, scientists are organized in distinct and incommensurable communities, each shaped by a different disciplinary matrix, and they work exclusively within the framework of this matrix. Only occasionally does a great upheaval take hold: old exemplars and models become invalid, well-established patterns of practice disappear, and boundaries between disciplines and specialties are redefined. Scientists then have to adapt to an entirely new way of perceiving their objects of study. Such a gestalt switch is often difficult.[46]

Knowing this, it is no wonder that scientists reject the idea of the Sasquatch because they prefer the comfort of familiar rather than new knowledge. They fail to push the boundaries of what they know because they are concerned with the potential difficulty of having to shift their perspective of the world.

Skeptics and scientists alike may argue that there is no Sasquatch paradox. They will point to evolution and argue that, although it became increasingly accepted, it was still largely considered to be nothing more than a pseudoscientific endeavor.

> Yet, however widespread these ideas (that is to say, beliefs about the fact of evolution) had become by the middle of the nineteenth century, it is fair to say they had but the status of quasi or pseudoscience, something akin to phrenology in those days and Scientology or transcendental meditation in our time. There were various reasons for the widespread nature of evolutionary beliefs and for their low status.[47]

This is, of course, a true and valid point to raise. However, it strengthens my argument as the debates and discussions that occurred with evolution have not yet happened. As we have seen, the evidence for a North American bipedal ape is overwhelming. You can argue that this is a natural part of the discovery process, but there has never been the same level of resistance to an idea as there is to the increasingly strong great ape hypothesis. Those who argue against the paradox fail to realize that "the success of an idea in science depends on many different factors."[48] As we can see, the evidence speaks for itself. However, there are other factors in the scientific community hindering this particular discovery. These factors are well within scientists' control: their preconceived notions. The failure of the scientific community to recognize the existence of Sasquatches, or at least to investigate it as a possibility, is nothing short of embarrassing.

Think back to Chapter 3's discussion of footprints. There, we learned of the work of the fingerprint experts who studied the footprint casts reportedly belonging to Sasquatches. They came to their conclusions after years in the classroom and many more in the field. As such, we would expect their testimony to hold weight among scientists. Sadly, this has not been the case.

> As with Krantz before him, Chilcutt's conclusions have been discussed with several of his associates in law enforcement, who have been very intrigued by the evidence. His preliminary findings have received typically guarded reactions from anthropologists and dermatoglyphists, even being denied an airing at some professional conferences. Certainly, they warrant further academic review. If repeated independent occurrences of dermatoglyphics in sasquatch footprint casts spanning several decades, with hundreds of miles of geographic separation, and displaying consistent yet distinct features of ridge texture and details of flow pattern can be confirmed, it would constitute compelling evidence for an unknown primate.[49]

If Chilcutt and other fingerprint experts had their expert testimonies, then it would be fair to ask if the criminals they help put behind bars should be released. Their opinions are clearly not as significant as we may believe if they are being routinely ignored.

Expanding on Tyson's idea (i.e., that believers should look for Sasquatch evidence). As alluded to above, people who do claim to have found evidence of Sasquatch tend to get ridiculed beyond belief. Skeptics, by ridiculing anyone who presents evidence, wonder with amazement how researchers claim that Sasquatches are real. This is similar to someone asking you for a favor, only to immediately criticize you once you have completed it. You are just completing the task that they asked you to complete. People who report sightings are doing their duty of reporting the very thing skeptics ask for: evidence (even if eyewitness evidence is anecdotal). Why should people be so vigorously attacked if they claim to have seen a Sasquatch? Surely, a well-educated skeptic would have more than enough knowledge to conduct a reasoned debate without resorting to the ever-low tactic of personal attack.

This chapter makes a bold claim about the Sasquatch paradox. However, when we strip away the mythical schema we hold of the ideals of the scientific community, we can see that the paradox, while not necessarily expected, is far from unanticipated. Scientists, both now and throughout history, have failed to live up to the ideals they claim to uphold. Yes, you have read this statement many times, but it must be repeated in order for you to comprehend the importance of its implications. Is it really likely that Sasquatches are the only issue facing artificial defiance? What else have we been told is an absolute fact by science that may, in fact, deserve to be reevaluated? Nowadays, scientific resistance has morphed into an artificial defiance that threatens to indefinitely stall the discovery of Sasquatches.

Having read this last chapter, you are much more likely to understand how a large bipedal ape could live in North America without having been discovered. We have a system that prevents evidence from emerging while simultaneously ridiculing and attacking anyone who attempts to investigate the issue. If the arguments made by Sasquatch researchers were so unsound, then they could easily and conclusively be destroyed in a serious scientific debate. However, such debates are prevented from occurring for the reasons outlined in this chapter. The discovery can only happen with the involvement of the scientific community. Without it, we will be left with an inexplicable set of authentic footprints left in the woods of North America.

From what we know about the scientific process, we can state that the best hypothesis makes the fewest assumptions. As such, we will now discuss the assumptions that underlie the arguments made by skeptics in order to conclusively understand why the hoax is the weaker of the two hypotheses. Doing this will allow us to fully comprehend the reality of the Sasquatch paradox. We must understand what arguments are made against the existence of Sasquatches, as well as the weaknesses of these arguments, in order to fully understand the artificial defiance against the existence of Sasquatches.

7

ASSUMPTIONS

At the beginning of *The Matrix*, Neo was initially hesitant when first offered the red pill but soon came to realize that he was being offered the truth. Knowing that his reality was merely an illusion allowed for him to ascend to his destiny of becoming the chosen one. Think of Neo's decision to take the red pill. Although fictional, we can still relate to the difficulty of being presented with evidence that contradicts what you previously held to be true. Neo was living in a world, which he felt was off, and wanted answers as to why he felt this way. Morpheus handed him the red pill, and that opened his eyes. The quote at the beginning of the book comes from this very scene in the film. Neo was given the opportunity to open his eyes and see the world for what it truly was.

You are in a similar position. You have been offered an explanation to a scientific mystery which, at first, seemed improbable. Just like Neo, you will soon be able to soar to new heights. Your eyes have been opened, but you still need more information. Neo triumphed not only because his eyes were opened but because he took the time to train and prepare. We must now follow Neo's example and work toward our understanding. We must now consider the arguments made against the existence of Sasquatches with our eyes fully open.

There are many arguments that are made against the great ape hypothesis. We will examine six of them in the following order: they are just misidentified bears (or other animals); if they were real, we would have more footage of them; if they were real, we would have found a body; if they are real, why is there so little evidence (which we have touched upon already); someone would have killed one with a car or a gun by now; and lastly, the environment cannot sustain their population. We will dissect each of these with our newfound awareness and systematically determine whether these arguments should be considered valid.

We talked in Chapter 1 (The Patterson-Gimlin Film) that there are some arguments that initially seem sound but lose their apparent strength upon closer inspection. Bears, as an explanation for Sasquatches, fall into this category. While it is true that bears do populate the majority of the areas where Sasquatches are seen, we have to remember that correlation is not causation. And yet, the skeptic might interject, they are both reported to be large, of a similar color, and bears can walk on their hind legs. All of those statements are true. However, we do not have to agree with the inference made by those skeptics. They are once again inferring causation from correlation. Animals are differently colored according to their regions. In fact, the differences in Sasquatch coloration over geographic distribution is exactly what we would expect to see in a living species.[1] As for their size, having two large-bodied species is insufficient in and of itself to claim that they would get confused for one another.

Bears can walk on their hind legs. This is a fact, much like the fact that the sun rises in the east. However, this does not mean that an upright bear looks like an ape. Bears can walk bipedally, but they move much more naturally as quadrupedal walkers. Indeed, they seldom take more than a few steps before dropping back down on all fours. One of the most frequently reported Sasquatch characteristics during encounters is that Sasquatches take long strides. We know that an ape the size of a Sasquatch would take long steps as they are reported to be over nine feet tall. This difference alone would make it difficult to confuse one for the other.

Bears have long snouts, flat heads, and long, pointy ears. Sasquatches, however, are reported as having flat faces, conically shaped heads, and ears that are rarely reported as being seen. Look at a gorilla, and you will see that there are strong similarities between their features and those reported of Sasquatches. Yes, correlation does not equal causation. However, the truth of both of these descriptions does help show that Sasquatches share strong similarities with other great apes.

Due to the abundance of nature documentaries, we are highly familiarized with bears and their appearance. Skeptics seem to forget this when making their bear claims. There is another important thing to consider: people may misidentify Sasquatches for bears. It is highly possible for people to make mistakes when they encounter an animal they do not recognize? Skeptics would interject here and say that believers are so desperate to experience encounters that they will warp an encounter with a bear into a Sasquatch. This is a statement I actually agree with. Many people imagine possible encounters to be absolute encounters due to wishful thinking. Moreover, Sasquatch searchers are not all experts with a high level of knowledge of the local fauna. These are all facts. We will examine more to see why the skeptics' claims are not fully true.

Most people do not believe in Sasquatches, and most people who encounter one did not believe prior to this experience. We will dive deeper into these two points to comprehensively understand the inaccuracy of skeptics' arguments. Before I do so, allow me to clarify something. While it is true that I agree with the skeptics' premise, I do not agree with their conclusion. That is why I simultaneously talk of agreeing and disagreeing with them. Yes, believers will warp an event to fit their perception of an encounter. However, it is important to remember that this also goes in the other direction. There are many people who see a Sasquatch who tell themselves they only saw a bear. I was once told of a man who would go alone to the woods of the Midwest. He placed trail cameras and would go to isolated locations that few individuals would be brave enough to go to. One night, he had an encounter. He saw something moving in a manner, unlike any other animal, while walking on two legs through a thermal imager. After that moment, the man, who had spent large amounts of time and money searching for Sasquatches, gave up his pursuit entirely. He told this story to my friend, much to his confusion. The man had told everyone that he had seen a bear. When questioned, the man responded along the lines that it is what he tells others and himself. His meaning was clear: his encounter had terrified him to the point that he began to lie to himself in order to gain some peace of mind.

As captivating as that tale is, we must remember that it is one story and we should not base anything significant on a small sample. However, it is telling that this man did the opposite of what skeptics argue: he tried to talk himself *out of* an encounter. This man was interested in the subject and was willing to talk about it. Following up on the second point, most people who encounter a Sasquatch did not believe in them beforehand. This seems reasonable as the population as a whole overwhelmingly does not believe in the existence of Sasquatches. Say you encounter an animal. That animal is large, covered in matter hair, and standing nine feet tall. You are a person that loves the outdoors: whether that be hunting, fishing, camping, or hiking. You do not want to give up a hobby you may have enjoyed for most of your life. After your encounter, you begin to question things. You cannot sleep, you are still in a state of shock. Then you tell yourself not to worry, it was only a bear after all. Are you telling yourself the truth? No, but the lie is easier than the truth. Moreover, no one will think that you are crazy for seeing an animal that people rarely believe in. Not only that, you no longer think that you are crazy as you yourself believe that Sasquatches cannot be real. Your eyes deceived you, or so you tell yourself. Ignorance is bliss. Better to lie so as to hide a traumatic event than face any possible repercussions.

Encountering a bear is a frightening event. Bears are extremely dangerous and can easily inflict the most dreadful (and often fatal) wounds. Bears can run and climb faster than humans and are also excellent swimmers. These skills, combined with their brute strength, make them animals to be wary of. However, due to our extensive knowledge of bears, we can be reassured that, both before and during an encounter, we can fully prepare. Imagine you see a bear in the woods. You are scared, but you are able to leave unscathed. You are more cautious in the future, but part of you liked the adrenaline rush you experienced. Furthermore, it becomes an excellent anecdote to tell. You, the brave person, facing down a monstrous animal makes for a captivating tale. However, what if you were to encounter an animal that you first believe to be a bear, but your common sense tells you that this is clearly not the case. It looks a lot more like an ape and a very tall one at that. You do not have that same feeling that you might have experienced from the bear encounter. Instead, you are terrified. You question reality, yourself, and the encounter. You have heard of other people encountering these same animals. However, you stay quiet as you fear the ridicule you would be subjected to. In fact, your kids, friends, or other family members may suffer ridicule as a result of your encounter. You decide to either keep quiet or tell people you saw a bear. Ignorance is bliss.

The above should help you put yourself in the shoes of someone who says they encountered a Sasquatch. We should concede that there are those who hold controversial opinions so that they can get attention from their strange beliefs. Look no further than the Flat Earth Society. Do you actually think that they truly believe the Earth is flat? It is much more likely that they hold this controversial opinion in order to gain attention. Think of it like peacocking. People wear vibrant clothes or accessories in order to stand out. The same is true of those who hold strong, unsubstantiated, and controversial opinions. Skeptics would argue that Sasquatches fall into this camp. However, after reading this book, you will know that this is not the case. You will have seen that there is sufficient evidence to suggest that Sasquatches exist. Continuing on, let us put ourselves in the shoes of someone who has encountered a Sasquatch. We know that people who make this claim face ridicule.

Do you think that those people are opening themselves up to ridicule because they want attention, or do you think they do so because of the firmness of their beliefs and desire for an explanation? When one encounters the unknown, the first thing that they attempt to do is explain it through the knowledge that they do possess. People know about bears, so they are likely to assume that they saw a bear, not a Sasquatch. Simply put, people are not confusing bears for Sasquatches. While there are some who may do this, there are many others who do the opposite; thereby significantly weakening the skeptics' claim.

While the arguments raised so far may be enough to convince some skeptics, they may still be wondering how Sasquatches can exist without us having found one. This is a question that should be asked. We should not go easy on believers. Indeed, we must put pressure on them to strengthen their arguments through research. There are far too many people who believe in Sasquatches for reasons outside of legitimate research. Too many people choose to believe first and only then search for facts (if at all). Instead, you should have an open mind, look for facts, and let them take you to the conclusion. This is true of all beliefs that people hold; indeed, simply think of people and their political opinions.

So you ask, how can one be real without us having found one? The answer is by no means straightforward, especially when we must first discuss what we mean by "found." Dr. John Bindernagel has an interesting take on the question. He argues that Sasquatches have already been found. What luck! Levity aside, Bindernagel argues that Sasquatches have already been discovered. His book, *The Discovery of the Sasquatch*, contains many detailed pieces of information that establish them as a real species. He argues that science is simply behind on the discovery. The discovery has already happened due to the encounters of countless individuals across North America. Admittedly, this is a bold claim, which means that I will now assume the burden of proof so as to convince you of it.

One of the most important things that Bindernagel uses as a premise for his argument is that the best hypotheses make the fewest assumptions.[2] He expands on this by including a quote from Richard Dawkins.

> The positive evidence in favour of the theory depends upon "parsimony": an economy of assumptions. A good theory is one that needs to postulate little in order to explain a lot.[3]

Dr. Bindernagel presents the great ape hypothesis as an alternative to the aforementioned hoax hypothesis. Skeptics, naturally, support the latter hypothesis, which "is based on the assertions of a few people who have claimed responsibility for either 'impersonating' a sasquatch in a film, or falsifying sasquatch tracks."[4]

Scientists will readily accept the hoax hypothesis due to its apparent plausibility. However, if they were to critique the hoax hypothesis as they do the great ape hypothesis, they would see that the former fails to stand up to any scrutiny. There are far too many unknowns in the hoax hypothesis for it to be accepted as valid. Imagine how difficult it would be for a few hoaxers to systematically leave (anatomically accurate) fake tracks and dress up in ape costumes to attempt to fool people into believing in Sasquatches. The hoax hypothesis significantly decreases in validity when we consider that there are features in the reported Sasquatch footprints that are consistent with other great apes: including midfoot flexibility, dermal ridges (which will curl properly toward wounds as they heal into scars), and sweat pores. We also have to consider the many military personnel, law enforcement members, and hunters who have claimed to have encountered a Sasquatch. Are we really going to consider a hypothesis valid that makes these two huge assumptions? Those assumptions being that there are hoaxers skilled enough to leave footprints of a high enough quality to fool anthropologists and dermal ridge experts and that there are hoaxers who can make such excellent quality costumes as to fool those trained to remember important details.[5] Of course, one could claim that the hoaxers lying rather than making the suits and footprints, but one would then have an additional assumption to explain.

Dr. Bindernagel notes that scientists will often ignore the anatomical details present in Sasquatch sightings. Instead, they argue against the existence of Sasquatches based on the notion "that there simply should not be a great ape in North America." Bindernagel continues this with, "In other words, whereas anatomical parsimony clearly indicates that the sasquatch is a member of a now-well described mammal group, the great apes, geographically parsimony argues against the occurrence of a nonhuman hominoid in North America."[6] Before we continue, it should be noted that ape fossils are not conducive to preservation. Apes live in areas that tend to receive significant amounts of precipitation and the ground in areas that receive a lot of rain are acidic, which makes it unlikely that the bones fossilize. It is well within reason that a great ape could live in North America and, due to the incomplete nature of the fossil record, have continued to live here without evidence from the fossil record.

The hoax hypothesis fails to fully explain the Sasquatch phenomenon because of the many assumptions that have to be made. The following are some of the biggest assumptions one would have to make: people are misidentifying bears as Sasquatches; people lie about encountering Sasquatches; there are teams of expert hoaxers placing anatomically correct footprints throughout the (most isolated) woods of North America to make their deception that much more believable; Roger Patterson had a secret ape suit making technique that he took to the grave; a Florida resident took a photo of an orangutan that was significantly larger than any of its kind; the forensic experts who identified dermal ridges on the footprint casts were all wrong; Drs. Krantz and Meldrum were wrong; the stories of Native American tribes, many of which relate to Sasquatch-like beings, should be considered just myths; and, lastly, North America cannot sustain a great ape population. These are all points that skeptics have to assume to be true; otherwise, their hypothesis is weakened beyond being useful. The above is a long list of very large assumptions that must be made. On the other hand, "The great ape hypothesis requires zoologists to make only two assumptions which go beyond current thinking: first, that a large, habitually bipedal great ape exists (other than humans), and second, that it occurs in North America."[7] Which hypothesis makes more assumptions: the hoax hypothesis or the great ape hypothesis? Remember Richard Dawkins' words, "A good theory is one that needs to postulate little in order to explain a lot."

Skeptics ask why we have not found a Sasquatch. Following Dr. Bindernagel's argument, we already have. Bindernagel argues that there is overwhelming evidence to suggest that Sasquatches are real animals. We will further this argument now as we discuss one person in particular who has scientific credibility and has had multiple encounters with Sasquatch-like-beings. That person is Gareth Patterson, the very same who helped rediscover the small population of Knysna elephants in South Africa. As he was conducting his search for these elusive animals, he happened upon an amazing animal, which the locals call the otang.

Already searching for an elusive animal, you can imagine the shock Patterson felt when he first encountered another. He encountered the otang early during his search for the Knysna elephants. During his time in South Africa, Patterson had a total of six sightings: two quick and four long. Having experience working with lions, Patterson knew how to maximize the length of his encounters. During one encounter, Patterson reported that looking at the animal directly would result in a limited duration. Instead, Patterson continued to walk, pretending not to see the otang while looking at it through his peripheral vision. This allowed him to accurately observe an otang, and what he saw was virtually identical to what people reported seeing in the North American woods. Patterson wrote about his encounters in his book *Beyond the Secret Elephants: On Mystery, Elephants, and Discovery*, which I would highly recommend.

One would assume that the fact that Patterson saw a relict hominid would result in scientific interest due to his credibility in the field. However, as you may have already guessed, there has been little interest in Patterson's story. Outside of a select few scientists, very little interest has been paid to his encounters. Patterson's work with the Knysna elephants (and previously with lions) should mean that his encounters would interest the scientific community. This is the type of person that the scientific community wants sightings from, or so they say, in order to take the subject seriously.[8] Patterson will be the only person with scientific credibility we will discuss but know that there are many more. Those with scientific credibility very rarely report their sightings. However, when they do, they do not want their name attached so as to protect their reputations.

Skeptics may concede that everything discussed in this section is convincing, but they may still be hesitant to believe due to the limited videos of Sasquatches. There are many reasons for the limited number of videos available. First, Sasquatches are elusive animals, thus being hard to find. Photographing such animals is easier said than done, which in itself might explain the lack of recent high-quality footage. This would also explain why a body has not been found. It is quite possible that Sasquatches have relatively low population numbers. Combine this with the fact that some elusive animals have enormous territories, we thus have a highly plausible explanation as to why they are rarely caught on film and why a body has not yet been found.

A further reason (hitherto unmentioned) also explains why we have yet to find one: Sasquatches are intelligent. Allow me to explain further. The intelligence of Sasquatches is a safe inference to make. There are strong parallels between Sasquatches and the known apes —who themselves are highly intelligent animals. However, it is possible that Sasquatches are more intelligent than other apes. Due to their sheer size, Sasquatches would sleep on the ground. We know from Sasquatch sightings that their size would eliminate an arboreal lifestyle. You would be right to question how sleeping on the ground would allow for Sasquatches to avoid detection.

Matthew Walker, in his book *Why We Sleep: Unlocking the Power of Sleep and Dreams*, presents a hypothesis that is of great interest to us. Walker details that, compared to other primates, humans are master sleepers. Our sleep is much more efficient: we sleep for shorter periods than other primates, and our rapid eye movement (REM) sleep is much more plentiful. The reason for our efficiency is simple: during REM sleep, "the brain paralyzes all voluntary muscles of the body, leaving you utterly limp."[9] REM is an essential part of sleep. The known great apes do not have so high a quality of sleep because they sleep in trees. While sleeping in trees is an excellent strategy to avoid predator attacks, it has a huge drawback: sleeping in trees reduces sleep efficiency. They sleep for longer but less deeply, and they spend considerably less time in REM sleep. Indeed, sleeping on the ground means that humans can let their bodies go limp at night without having to worry about falling to the ground. Dr. Walker goes as far as to argue that sleeping on the ground is what allowed Homo sapiens to leap to the top of the food chain. The REM sleep, and dreaming, that comes from getting higher quality sleep has significantly increased "our degree of sociocultural complexity, and our cognitive intelligence." It follows that an ape, which is already considered one of the smartest animals, would become more intelligent just from sleeping on the ground.[10]

What if we are not the only ape to sleep on the ground. Based on Walker's theories, it would be safe to assume that any ape that slept on the ground would stand to gain the similar benefits of deep sleep as humans. More and deeper REM leads to higher critical thinking skills.

> REM sleep and the act of dreaming have another distinct benefit: intelligent information processing that inspires creativity and promotes problem-solving... Deep REM sleep strengthens individual memories... But it is REM Sleep that offers the masterful and complimentary benefits of fusing and blending those elemental ingredients together (creativity and problem solving) in abstract and novel ways.[11]

This theory, when taken into account with what we have learned about Sasquatches, assumes very little in order to explain a lot. It provides a probable explanation as to why Sasquatches could have been able to avoid humans while only assuming their existence and size.

Furthermore, we have to remember that animals do become used to other animals, including humans. Animals adapt to their environment and competitors. "Niche partitioning—when coexisting species avoid competing with each other by behaving or feeding in slightly different ways."[12] Maybe the reason that Sasquatches are nocturnal—which we can infer from the majority of sightings occurring at night—comes from this niche partitioning. It is very reasonable to infer that Sasquatches became nocturnal to avoid competition with bears. Additionally, we can also safely say that if Sasquatch lived alongside humans for upwards of 10,000 years, it is highly likely that they would have learned to do so effectively. Moreover, it would be reasonable to assume that they have learned ways to avoid humans. As stated above, Sasquatches are smart. Animals of lesser intelligence avoid humans out of fear for their safety. It is only fair to argue the same thing would be true of Sasquatches. The difference is simple: Sasquatch would have the added benefit of coming from a more intelligent branch of the tree of life and would further have this intelligence exponentially improved with the added benefit of more efficient and deep REM sleep. Nocturnal activity would help them to avoid humans. Being a smarter ape active during the night helps explain why they have not yet been found.

The third assumption can be viewed as an extension of the previous one: why have more Sasquatches not been filmed? While we have already discussed why Sasquatches are a hard species to find, we will now detail why filming one is harder than one might think. There are two different arguments made by skeptics in this regard: everyone nowadays carries a camera with them in their pocket, and the wilderness is full of thousands of trail cameras. Filming one during an encounter might sound like a natural or obvious thing to do, yet it is much harder than it sounds. Imagine the following scenario: while walking in the woods, you notice a strange feeling. Then you remember that you forgot your favorite camera at home, but, no worries, your smartphone takes fairly high-quality photos. As you are walking, you cannot help but think how beautiful it is in the woods. The birds are chirping, and the wind is blowing. Too bad you are a bit distracted from the worries of everyday life to notice that the birds have fallen silent. You turn a corner and what do you find? A nine-foot-tall ape staring directly at you. You are so close you seem sure it could reach out and touch you. The first thought racing through your mind is, *what am I looking at*? You ask more questions, *Is this real, am I safe, should I run?* All this time, your mind is processing the situation as fast as possible in order to determine the course of action which leads to survival.

Five seconds feels like an hour. You are frozen with fear. That is until you decide escape is the best possible option. You run. Your adrenaline is pumping, your heart is racing faster than it ever has done before. Suddenly, you stop. You remember that you are carrying a smartphone, your very own portable camera. Hesitation grips you as you are unsure if returning is the best idea. You ready your camera and return to the spot. You find nothing, only the returning sound of birds chirping.

I can assure you that taking a photo in one of these situations is much harder said than done. You could argue that the above scenario is extremely plausible and does explain why photos are not always taken, but what about those who are out specifically searching for Sasquatches? We would expect them to take a wealth of photos. I ask you this: can you truly prepare yourself for seeing an ape that grows nearly twice as tall as the average man? An acquaintance of mine once ventured out on an expedition to find a Sasquatch. There he was, positioning himself for an encounter, camera at the ready. During the day, he went off on his own to eat his lunch away from everyone else. Suddenly, a group of deer ran at him. Startled, he ran toward the direction they came from to see what had caused the commotion. There, standing in front of him, was a six-foot-tall figure.

Surely he must have taken a picture? No, he ran, even though he had a camera and the very thing that scared him was exactly what he was searching for. Additionally, this man has been out in the woods many times and conducts himself in a highly professional manner in the field. He is far from the average layperson in the woods. There is no way to mentally prepare oneself for encountering these animals. In fact, it is likely to happen when you least expect it. Skeptics may read this section and think that the argument is sound. You might think that the above scenarios explain the lack of pictures. However, you say, I cannot wrap my head around the fact that there are no trail camera photos. If they were real, we would expect to see such photos.

The Siberian tiger would serve as an excellent example here. As mentioned, they are elusive, dangerous, and live over huge territories. Naturally, we would assume that positioning trail cameras would be the best way to find them. However, tigers are not so easily fooled. Amazingly, not only do tigers recognize trail cameras, they know how to destroy them without being caught on camera. The tigers go behind the cameras, bite the strap holding it to the tree, and then destroy the now facedown camera.[13] Not only will they destroy these cameras, but they will also destroy guns that are set out as traps. The guns are set to fire once something triggers a rope. The tigers have learned to destroy these traps, even to the point of setting the gun off first so as to reduce any harm to them.[14] If tigers can avoid these traps, surely apes (as some of the smartest creatures alive) can do so as well. Apes could very easily stay clear of the camera traps laid out across the North American wilderness. Taking into account their greater intelligence as a result of their more efficient sleep, we can see why the odds of filming one are near zero.

The fourth assumption has already been covered through discussing the second. The fourth assumption is that we should have found a dead Sasquatch by now. This has been discussed in enough detail that we do not need to repeat it here. However, there is one aspect to it that we should discuss before continuing to the fifth assumption. We, skeptics and believers alike, assume that bones are easily identifiable. However, this is not necessarily the case. A geology student once found a fossil of a Triassic amphibian. However, he was unaware of its importance, and the bone sat in a museum unattended for nearly 30 years.[15] Just because a bone is found does not mean that it will attract the attention that it deserves, nor even that it would be properly identified. Think back to footprints. There are footprints that show anatomical details that would be impossible to fake, yet they are ignored because scientists cannot comprehend their true importance. In a perfect world, finding a bone would help prove the species' existence. Unfortunately, we live in the real world, where good evidence can—and does—get overlooked.

The fifth assumption is that someone would have killed one by now. There are enough differences between this assumption and the second, third, and fourth so as to merit separate discussion. Just killing one of these animals would be enough to prove their existence. Doing so would end the debate. In fact, the North American wilderness is filled with hunters. Some feel that this means we can safely assume that a hunter would have encountered a Sasquatch by now. Indeed, these hunters could potentially make a fortune from killing a Sasquatch. However, again, doing so is actually much less simple and needs more in-depth analysis.

Shooting and killing an animal is far from easy. The most basic instinct an animal has is its instinct for survival. Wild animals live difficult lives, making them expert survivors. Most animals will avoid putting themselves in situations where they can be easily attacked or killed. The reason hunters are able to kill most animals is because these animals become vulnerable during their mating seasons. Animals are so preoccupied with mating that they reduce their levels of alertness. It also is true that there are millions of deer, turkeys, and other animals that are hunted each year. Of course, animals lower down on the food chain have much greater populations than those higher up.

Skeptics could refute this by saying that the above is not truly pertinent. Skeptics could argue that I have said that Sasquatch encounters happen more often than reported, meaning that we should also expect more hunters to have encountered these creatures than reported. They could continue their argument by saying that one of the most often reported encounters are roadside encounters. We should expect there to have been one killed on the road. These are perfectly reasonable rebuttals and are worth discussing in detail. We have to understand that there are many different hunting seasons that require different types of weaponry used to hunt the target animal. Different weapons are used on different animals for a multitude of reasons. First, you do not want to shoot an animal with too large a round so as not to damage the meat. However, too small a round risks causing injury to the animal without necessarily killing it. An injured animal can be particularly dangerous to the hunter who just shot it.

Ammunition itself has risen dramatically in price, meaning that hunters would prefer not to waste it. Not every hunter sets off with a gun powerful enough to kill an animal the size of a Sasquatch. Most hunters actually use guns that are too small to be considered a reliable caliber to kill an animal that large. A large animal that gets shot will potentially turn on the person who shot it in order to eliminate the threat to its survival. As a hunter, you know the type of weapon that you are carrying, which is likely to use smaller rounds than those required to kill a nine-foot-tall ape. Put yourself in a hunter's shoes. You are in the woods. The gun you have is anywhere between a .22 and a .338. The former is for smaller animals and the latter for larger. Say you have the larger of those two guns, the .338. You are ready to shoot a whitetail deer, which you are perfectly capable of doing. However, that plan is quickly derailed when you see something odd, albeit much larger than your target animal.

You believe that your mind is playing tricks on you, but the longer the encounter lasts, the more you realize that your eyes are not deceiving you. You pull up your gun. You want to pull the trigger as you know the fame and fortune this animal's body would bring. Instead of shooting the animal, you lower your gun. Your decision to shoot was twofold: the immense size of the animal was enough to cause you to second guess your gun, and the animal showed too much resemblance to a human to be shot. Your gun, while of great service to you during your time hunting, was simply too small to have been able to down the animal. Of course, even if you had had a gun big enough to have killed what you just saw, you likely would still not have pulled the trigger. The animal looked too human-like. You know in your heart that the animal was not human, but it looked just human enough to make you pause and ask if killing one would be to commit murder. Furthermore, perhaps you feared the possible repercussions of killing an animal out of season.

On the surface, one would think that hunters would kill one. However, we know now that this is less likely than it first appears to be. As for the claim that a Sasquatch should have been hit by a car by now, a different approach is required. Drive in a rural area and you are bound to see dead animals alongside the road. These animals are usually either deer, raccoons, or possums. We see that these animals are frequently at the losing end of a one-sided fight with cars. The main reason we see these animals dead by the side of the road is because of their enormous population numbers. There are more of them to get hit than animals higher up on the food chain. Where I grew up, there are very few bears, meaning that there are even fewer bears lying dead alongside the road. The lower the number of a certain animal in an area, the lower the odds one will get hit by a car. There have been hundreds, if not thousands, of deer, raccoons, or possums that have been hit and killed along the roadside near my house in the 20 years I have been living there. In that time, only one bear has been hit and killed.

Sasquatches are extraordinary animals in that their intelligence is greater than that of the other great apes. Moreover, being at the top of the food chain, they have small population numbers. Ecosystems simply cannot maintain as many top predators as they can animals lower down the food chain. Both of these facts plausibly explain why they do not get hit and killed by cars. However, these are not the only two facts to consider. We should note that there are people who have claimed to hit a Sasquatch. Now, we must ask two questions here: did these collisions actually happen, and were they reported to their insurance companies? If not, then we have nothing further to discuss. If so, then we must delve a little deeper into the claim. Sasquatches are reported as growing to exceptionally large sizes, meaning that any vehicle colliding with one would suffer the consequences. Although some have claimed to have had such collisions, we can safely assume that the majority of people (if they truly did hit one) would not report it to their insurance companies out of fear of not being reimbursed.

The sixth and last assumption we will discuss is that the environment cannot sustain its population. On the surface, this assumption is the weakest of the six. There are many ways we can further weaken this assumption. First and foremost, if North America can support a large number of bears throughout its vast territory, then it is conceivable that it can support other large omnivores. There are more than enough streams, lakes, and rivers to provide Sasquatches with water. Furthermore, there are more than enough crops, animals, and vegetation to provide Sasquatches with food. There are many exceptionally large animals in North America: elk, moose, bison, and grizzly bears, for instance. We would assume that if the environment could not sustain a Sasquatch population, then it would be unable to do so for these species as well. Moreover, Sasquatches are said to be omnivorous, meaning that they would have a larger selection of food than the three herbivorous animals above (excluding the grizzly bear).

Sasquatch sightings from around North America actually tell us more than what most people realize. The above-listed six assumptions are part of the hoax hypothesis. While we have previously explained the hypothesis, it is worth repeating that it states that the Sasquatch phenomenon can be explained by hoaxes and misidentifications. We must remember that to retain any of its apparent strength, the hoax hypothesis needs all of these assumptions to be true. The hoax hypothesis continues with one last assumption: hoaxers help explain Sasquatch. As such, we would expect that there would be a great degree of randomness (typically absent in the natural world) with the hoaxed sightings and footprints. The most plausible scenario (of a highly implausible group) for explaining the hoax hypothesis is that there are individuals or small teams around North America hoaxing Sasquatch evidence. The other option is that there is a single team of hoaxers who systematically plan everything. We know that this is unlikely because of the difficulties people have in maintaining secrecy. Indeed, within such a large group, at least one person would talk. Keeping such a giant team quiet would cost a considerable amount of money and would require an enormous amount of time and effort from everyone involved. Thus, the only possible scenario that the hoax hypothesis works is that there are individuals who routinely fake Sasquatch evidence. For argument's sake, we can assume that these would conceivably be smaller working teams.

Moving forward with this idea, we can safely assume that Sasquatch reports and footprints would be varied to the point of random, which is not seen in nature. Although there are some variations among reports, the random variation we would expect of the hoaxers does not occur as we would expect. Indeed, the variations actually tell a very interesting story. First, the footprints become larger as they go further north, thereby following Bergmann's Rule. This scientific law states that an animal of the same species grows larger the further north it lives, as larger animals conserve heat more easily. This is why polar bears are so much larger than black bears. They have to be larger in order to conserve energy more efficiently. If we accept the hoax hypothesis, we also have to accept that there would be randomness within the evidence. Since the opposite is true (especially with the footprint casts), the hoax hypothesis as a viable theory becomes significantly weaker. The reason we can make this statement is that a small team of hoaxers would, in all probability, use footprint casts of the same size, as this would be both cheaper and easier than the alternative. There could conceivably be individuals going out into the woods planting fake prints. Allow me to reiterate a quote from Napier: "who other than God or natural selection is sufficiently conversant with the subtleties of the human foot and the human walking style to 'design' an artificial foot which is so perfectly harmonious in terms of structure and function?" Now, let me put a twist on this quote in order for it to better fit the hoax assumption. Who other than God or natural selection could place footprints in woods in a way that perfectly follows this little-known (Bergmann's Rule) scientific law?

Not only do footprints follow scientific rules, but so does fur color. George Gil, an anthropologist, found that:

> Perhaps it should be mentioned at this point that during the screening of Sasquatch reports it appeared as though not only size but also coat colour varied in similar fashion from south to north. Coat colour variations do exist within mammalian species, and they do often vary by latitude. This zoological principle is sometimes referred to as Gloger's Rule, and holds that darker shades tend to occur more frequently in moister, warmer regions (such as the more southerly zones in North America) and that blonder tones are more frequent in cooler, drier places... the majority in Washington and Canada are reported as brown, reddish, or black, but the much larger percentage of light coat colours in the north may be significant.[16]

Indeed, this was so convincing to Gil that he came to the following conclusion:

> The two possible explanations for our results: 1. That the most complex and sophisticated hoax in the history of anthropology has continued for centuries without being exposed; 2. That the most manlike (and largest) non-human primate on earth has managed to survive in parts of North America and remains undiscovered by modern science. Either conclusion appears totally preposterous in light of the problem-solving capability of modern science; yet, one of these two possible conclusions must be true.[17]

Gil found this after realizing the high levels of consistency among

Sasquatch reports. In fact, they follow ecogeographical rules. Who other than God or natural selection could place footprints in such a way that perfectly follows Bergmann's Rule, while sightings simultaneously follow Gloger's Rule, another little-known rule that details coat color variations? We expect to see variations like this in a living species. "Precise uniformity within a species is not a characteristic of nature, whereas variety is."[18]

For those who still need to be convinced that North America can sustain a population of large bipedal apes, Dr. Krantz can best explain North America's suitability. In an article written for *The Scientist Looks at the Sasquatch*, Krantz argued that development in the 19th and 20th centuries inadvertently made the land more suitable for large mammals through the destruction of mature forests (which are known to have relatively few resources compared to new growth forests). "Most large species of herbivores and omnivores depend largely on second-growth following deforestation for their best foraging—mature forests being notably inedible."[19] Additionally, humans have done an excellent job of eradicating the Sasquatch's most fierce competitor, the grizzly bear. Both of these facts serve to explain how Sasquatches could not only still be alive today but possibly thriving.[20] We thus see how the skeptic claim that North America is inhospitable crumbles in the face of scrutiny. Indeed, it seems that human expansion throughout North America has been a net benefit for Sasquatches due to the reduction in the number of its competitors. In fact, there are likely fewer black bears, mountain lions, and wolves of which to compete with, so the Sasquatch has gained quite the upper hand.

There is one last important argument made by skeptics that must be addressed before we discuss the poor arguments proposed by believers. Skeptics will disbelieve any reports by those claiming to have seen a Sasquatch while simultaneously being ready and willing to listen to anything a hoaxer says. Hoaxers occasionally admit to their misdeeds, which skeptics use as evidence for the hoax hypothesis. However, they make a major contradiction in doing so. They take as viable evidence the word of someone who admits to having lied about this subject. Why then should we trust these hoaxers? They are known liars, meaning that taking their word at face value is perplexing, especially as these same skeptics would level this charge at anyone who claimed to have encountered a Sasquatch. Needless to say, it is best not to give hoaxers the oxygen of attention. We should not give these liars the very thing that they want.

Although it may initially seem as if the arguments made by skeptics are sound, we now know this is not to be the case. Needless to say, it is important for us to recognize bad arguments in order to conclusively settle the Sasquatch question. It is pertinent for us to also discuss the bad arguments put forward by believers, and we would be remiss if we neglected to do so. There are just as many, if not more, bad arguments on this side of the debate. In order to conduct ourselves in a scientific manner, we must recognize and fix the mistakes we make. We would not be any better than the scientists we criticize if we pretended that only skeptics make bad arguments about Sasquatches.

Arguably the most common bad argument made by believers comes when they attribute any and every sound in the woods to Sasquatches. To illustrate this point, allow me to tell a story. After the lockdown (as a result of the COVID-19 pandemic), many people were ready to make it back into the woods. Unfortunately, the 2020 Wisconsin BFRO trip was canceled, but where there is a will, there is a way. An unofficial trip to the large and beautiful southwest Wisconsin took its place. After meeting with a few BFRO members, our plan was to walk into the woods on a trail in the hope of a possible Sasquatch encounter. As we began our walk, it soon dawned on me that the group was too inexperienced in the woods to make objective decisions as to what had made a certain sound. Our group heard a noise in the distance. I believed that it was simply too far for any of us to accurately determine what had made the sound. The other members of the group were certain it was a Sasquatch. Indeed, they even said as much to other members who we met with on the next night.

In terms of experience in the woods, I had the most out of the first night's group. I grew up close to this location and have spent over a decade hunting deer. Needless to say, my input should not have been ignored. There are certain signs that a top predator is in an area. One such sign is that nearby animals fall silent as the top predator approaches. Naturally, animals do not want to attract a potential threat to their location. When we heard that distant sound, frogs and other animals were still clearly making noise. This location is somewhat close to a road and contains many camping locations. That sound could have been anything at all. There was simply not enough information to have inferred the presence of a Sasquatch.

Studying for the LSAT helped me greatly improve my logical reasoning ability. Moreover, it has also helped me recognize bad arguments. One of the question types in the logical reasoning section comes in the form of an inference. We are asked to determine which of the five answer choices best support the information in the passage. Say we are told, "Most people hate rain. Most people who hate rain also prefer driving to walking. Sandra hates rain." We would then be presented with five answer choices and told to choose the correct one. They may look like: A. Sandra hates walking, B. Most people prefer driving over walking, C. There are more people who like sunshine than rain, D. People who prefer to drive do so because they do not like wearing raincoats, and E. Some people do not hate rain. While this is a very simplified version of what one might see on the LSAT, it serves to explain the logical reasoning process.

The correct answer is E. A. is wrong because it could be true, but we cannot make this inference based solely on the information provided. We know that most people hate rain, of which Sandra falls under this category. We know most people who hate rain prefer driving to walking. However, we do not know if Sandra falls under either those who prefer driving or those who prefer walking. B. is wrong because we know almost nothing about most people, only that most of them hate the rain. "Most" means the majority, meaning this could either be 99% or 51%. If 51% (or the majority) of the population hate rain, of that 51%, 26% could prefer driving. Therefore, it is possible that only those 26% prefer driving. While it could certainly be true that most people prefer driving, it does not have to be true based on the information given to us. For C., we do not have enough information to determine its validity. It could be true, but it is not supported by the information in the passage. The passage makes no mention of people who like sunshine, only about those who hate rain. D., we know that there are some people who prefer driving over walking, but we are not told why. Nowhere are we given information as to why they have this preference. E. is correct because it is the only one that we can properly infer based on what we are told. Most people hate rain means that at least 51% hate rain. It could be more, it could be 99%, or it could be 51%. We know it is not 100%, because otherwise, the question would have told us that all people hate rain. That means that there is part of the population that does not hate rain. We do not know how many. All we know is that most, but not all, hate rain. Some means at least one, which would cover the missing portion of the population. This is the only answer we can choose without making an improper inference. It is the only inference we can make from the information we are provided with.

Many LSAT answer choices are wrong because they say something that could be true but does not necessarily have to be. We can only infer from the information provided in the question. It is possible that most people hate walking due to their dislike of raincoats, but that does not have to be true. The same applies to those members of the group who cried Sasquatch. It could have been a Sasquatch, but it is highly improper to make this inference due to the lack of evidence and the abundance of alternate explanations.

Another commonly made argument by believers is that Sasquatches possess the ability to make their eyes glow red. This is an unusual argument as these same believers claim that Sasquatches want to remain elusive, but at the same time, will give away their position by making their eyes glow red. The problem with this theory —and many others presented by believers and skeptics alike—is that it is based solely on belief. These people believe in something and look for evidence to validate their argument. Indeed, they do the opposite of what the scientific process outlines. The scientific process is supposed to help prevent confirmation bias. However, this can only be done if people follow the process properly.

Two more bad arguments made by believers are that Sasquatches are interdimensional beings and that the government is covering up their existence. The former can safely be dismissed out of hand and requires no further discussion. The latter, however, is worth some of our attention. People today are very conspiratorial. As such, people are increasingly willing to believe in a conspiracy where one does not exist. Moreover, our culture is filled with movies and books about one lone truth seeker unraveling government conspiracies. People like to assume that they are equally adept at finding conspiracies as their favorite fictional characters. Unfortunately for these people, fiction is different from reality. The government has absolutely no reason to cover up the existence of Sasquatches. If they did want to hide their existence, do you really think that you would be reading this book right now? The main reason that believers make these arguments is because they reject the scientific community. Indeed, this results in the proposal of theories completely ungrounded in reality.

As we can see, both sides of the debate propose bad arguments. It is important to eliminate bad arguments so as to protect the subject as a whole. Believers do not realize those poor arguments negatively affect those who are following the scientific process. Skeptics making bad arguments may not hurt the skeptical community in the same way as the bad arguments of believers, but negative effects still result from this. Skeptics can become so skeptical that they completely close their minds to any new ideas, which can cause them to be so stubborn in their beliefs that they miss out on valuable information.

After reading up to this point in the book, you may be asking yourself how we might overcome this artificial defiance? Although the Sasquatch paradox is complex, the cure is actually quite simple.

8

THE CURE

Few people give enough respect to mechanics. Ensuring that our cars run smoothly is a necessity of life. Without our cars, we would be unable to get where we need to go with ease. While there are many people who live in areas with public transportation, there are many more who do not have this option available to them. Thus, cars must be kept in optimal conditions. The difference between a working and malfunctioning car in terms of the effect on one's stress levels is highly significant. Mechanics are the doctors of cars. Granted, they may not have to undergo the same level of professional preparation, but they still help impact one of the often overlooked aspects of our lives. Mechanics are truly amazing. Recently, my mechanic was able to diagnose the problem with my car after only a handful of descriptions. He then recommended the proper solution to ensure that my car could continue to run in perfect condition.

Doctors share certain similarities to mechanics. Having a car breakdown is very troublesome and can negatively impact someone's life (as well as their bank account). However, there is something reassuring about the fact that your car can get new parts. If the new parts do not solve the issue, replacement cars are readily available. The human body is much more delicate than a car. If your body breaks down, the odds are against you being able to find a replacement.

Doctors must be able to quickly ascertain what is wrong with their patients so as to determine the best course of action for future treatment. The vast amount of time spent in training allows doctors to do this. In this manner, the diagnostic aspect is similar between doctors and mechanics. The similarities between the two professions do not end there. Both contain those who work under the guise of having a broad knowledge of a lot of issues, and both have those who specialize in certain areas of interest. When the clutch of my truck broke, it was a huge relief to be able to take it to a transmission expert who fixed it quickly and for an extremely fair price. When my hip was out of alignment due to a four-wheeling accident, I was extremely fortunate to be able to hire a physical therapist who was able to put it back into place with the simplest of exercises.

We have so far discussed only the symptoms of the ailment currently affecting the scientific community. We would be remiss if we failed to talk about the cure. What good would our doctors and mechanics be if they told us the problem but not the solution? The problem of artificial defiance in the scientific community is a major problem. Our transmission is leaving our car. However, although the problem is serious and will resolving, the issue can be fixed with relative ease. When my hip was out of alignment, I feared that surgery would be the only answer: which could potentially have resulted in debilitating lower back and hip problems that would impact me for the rest of my life. Needless to say, when the physical therapist fixed my hip with three simple exercises, I was majorly relieved.

That said, sometimes a large problem only needs a small change to be fixed. The same is true for artificial defiance: it is a complicated problem with a simple solution. We only need there to be scientific interest in the subject of Sasquatch and the problem should then fix itself. My physical therapist told me that my back should heal as long as I continue to do the recommended exercises and avoid unnecessary strain on my lower back. That same theory applies here:

artificial defiance can be eradicated as long as the scientific community truly examines the issue with an open mind. It truly is as simple as that. You may be asking yourself, how can it be that this issue can be solved so easily? Allow me to demonstrate how this has worked in other scientific fields.

To the chagrin of many movie fans, I think that *Jurassic Park* is an overrated movie. While it was my favorite movie as a kid, and the adult in me can recognize its truly impressive scenes, the movie is just filled with too many mistakes. None bigger than the fact that velociraptors are so poorly depicted. They did not grow as large as they are shown to grow. Also, a Tyrannosaurus Rex would certainly not expend significant calories on chasing humans when humans would provide it with minimal calories.

Most of us, myself included love dinosaurs. As I grew older, the accuracy of the facts presented in dinosaur movies became increasingly important to me. Indeed, that makes it very hard to watch any dinosaur movie as Hollywood prefers drama over accuracy. That presents quite the dilemma: how do people who love dinosaurs, but champion accuracy, indulge in their need for dinosaur entertainment? This question perplexed me until I stumbled upon the many books written on the subject at a bookstore. Seeing a dinosaur book on a shelf that day represented a must-buy. Needless to say, the book was filled with fascinating information. None more so than the fact that there was a lull in dinosaur discoveries in the 1970s.

The first dinosaur bones were quite the find. Try to imagine how the discovery of one bone was enough to completely change how people thought of prehistory. Many of us would assume that this would automatically result in scientific interest in the subject: which is partially true, but it was not a continuous interest. Dinosaurs were a popular topic when the first bones were found in the late 19th century, and the interest associated with them continued for many decades. However, this was to die down. It went from being a topic that held the allure of the scientific community to one which was soon overlooked. So it should come as no surprise that important discoveries went ignored.

The discovery of dinosaur bones by a local rancher in Argentina represented was a significant event, though less so for the scientific community as you would expect.[1] "You might think this discovery would have encouraged paleontologists from throughout Argentina... There was little funding and, believe it or not, little public interest."[2] Little funding and little public interest were enough to stall discoveries of dinosaur fossils. If these factors were enough to halt further discoveries in such a popular field, consider what effect little funding and the public interest would have on a less popular topic.

We assume that people were as interested in dinosaurs as we are today, yet this was not the case. Dinosaur fossils in the 1960s and '70s are analogous to the search for Sasquatches today. Although evidence was still being found, the discovery process was stalled due to the lack of interest from the scientific community and public alike. However, once the public interest picked up, so did the scientific interest. Funding was set aside for expeditions after the 1970s, which led to more discoveries in the field of paleontology. We may believe dinosaurs to be fascinating, but we should remember that not everyone shares (or shared) this same interest.

The power of both scientific and public interest can have an exponential effect on discovery. Look no further than the COVID-19 pandemic. We were sure that we were going to be locked down for all of 2020 and beyond (15 days to flatten the curve). We were told by the former president of the United States that a vaccine would be available in 2020, but did anyone believe him? Part of the president's job is to reassure the American people. We believed his comment to be nothing more than false hope. Needless to say, that slight glimmer of hope has manifested into a general return to normality of a kind. Never has a vaccine been created so quickly. Universal interest and unlimited funding helped researchers develop a number of vaccines, which they did by the end of 2020. We are certainly fortunate in the variety of vaccines available. In case one vaccine may have been ineffective, there were multiple others that could be used instead. Do you think that we would have developed a vaccine so quickly if there had been no interest from the public/scientific community? Of course not. This is just the most modern-day example of interest helping to further the discovery process.

Looking back at Gareth Patterson's story on the Knysna elephants, we can see just how powerful scientific interest in a subject truly is. The park workers were keen on the elephants' survival as it was an important aspect of their life. Using their knowledge gave Patterson an advantage as compared to going in blind. Talking to a forest worker, Patterson asked how elephants could survive for so long without having been found. A veteran worker replied, "The forests are very big... and though elephants are huge, the forests make them small by comparison."[3] When there was a sighting of these elusive large animals, the excitement in the area was hard to contain. A photograph of a bull sparked excitement and generated increased public and scientific interest.[4]

Patterson had help when looking for the elephants. He had interested geneticists on hand who agreed to test elephant DNA. With their help, the elephants' discovery inched ever closer to its conclusion.[5] The DNA analysis of the fecal matter from the elephants gave Patteson much-needed information as to the number and sex of the elephants in the area. Needless to say, the scientific interest helped solve this issue. We can infer that this same interest would also have translated into increased conservation and protection efforts.

The theory of evolution was accepted as valid after many years of fierce debate (and slander, of course). Even after it was determined to be valid, there were still questions surrounding the theory. However, scientists took the time to discuss the theory amongst themselves. The theory was of interest and time was spent considering it from every possible angle, through every possible lens. We would not have the detailed knowledge of evolution without there has been interest from the scientific community.

Thomas Kuhn argued that scientific attention was a key phase in the discovery process:

> Discovery commences with the awareness of [an] anomaly, i.e., with the recognition that nature has somehow violated the paradigm-induced expectations that govern normal science. It then continues with a more or less extended exploration of the area of anomaly. And it closes only when the paradigm theory has been adjusted so that the anomalous has become the expected.[6]

Scientific interest is a stepping stone that must occur to make discovery possible. Without interest, you are left with books like this trying to uncover a phenomenon that could have been discovered long ago. The only thing that would have been—and still is—needed to prompt the discovery of the Sasquatch is scientific interest.

9

CONCLUSION

For this final chapter, instead of me reiterating the contents of this book in a systematic rehash of previously provided information, we will go with a different approach. The approach is simple: I will pose questions for you. You will not have to leaf through past chapters to answer these questions. They are much simpler and only require a "yes" or "no."

Could the Patterson-Gimlin Film have been hoaxed with the technology available in 1967?

Is the Myakka ape an orangutan?

Are there dermal ridges on reported Sasquatch plaster casts?

Were these dermal ridges verified as authentic by experts?

Do native tribes have stories of Sasquatch?

Do some of these same tribes have carved stone heads or masks depicting apes?

Is it likely that the African apes could have influenced these tribes?

Is it acceptable to openly discuss Sasquatches as a scientist?

Is there a history of scientific failure with regards to discovery?

Are scientists living up to their ideals?

Does the great ape hypothesis make fewer assumptions than the hoax hypothesis?

Are people confusing bears for Sasquatches?

Who other than God could place footprints in the woods of North America that follow Bergmann's Rule while at the same time having sightings that follow Gloger's Rule? No further questions.

AFTERWORD

Readers will, of course, decide for themselves just where the claim of discovery for the sasquatch belongs... But no matter how scientific colleagues and scientifically minded readers perceive the discovery claim—whether they view it as interesting, suggestive, persuasive, compelling, or obvious—sasquatches, which evidently do inhabit many parts of North America, will continue to leave tracks and other physical sign, challenging scientific orthodoxy, and confirming the species' existence, even if its discovery remains unacknowledged.[1]

PHOTO INDEX

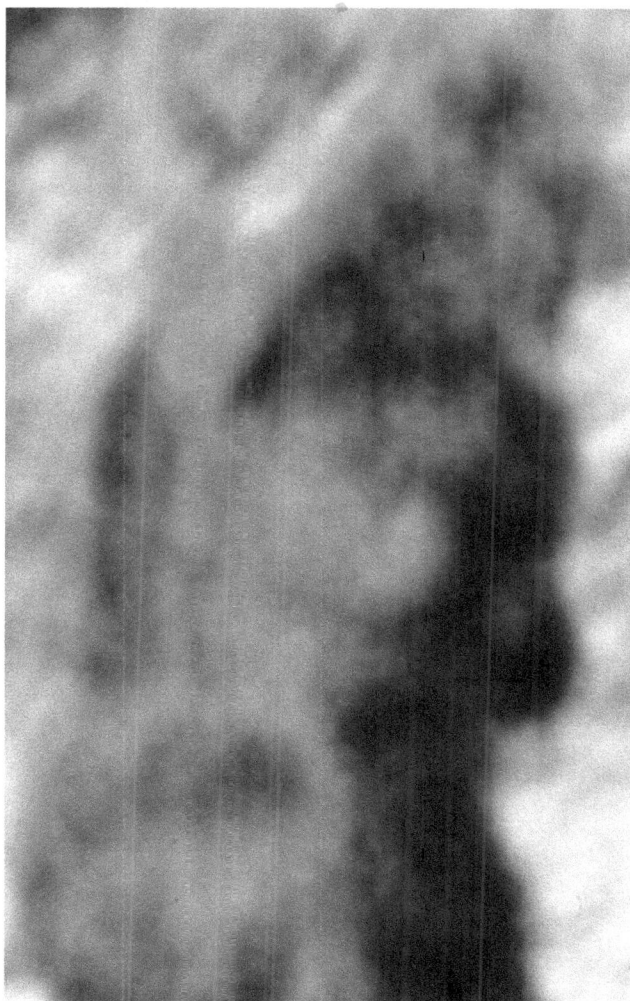

Fig. 1

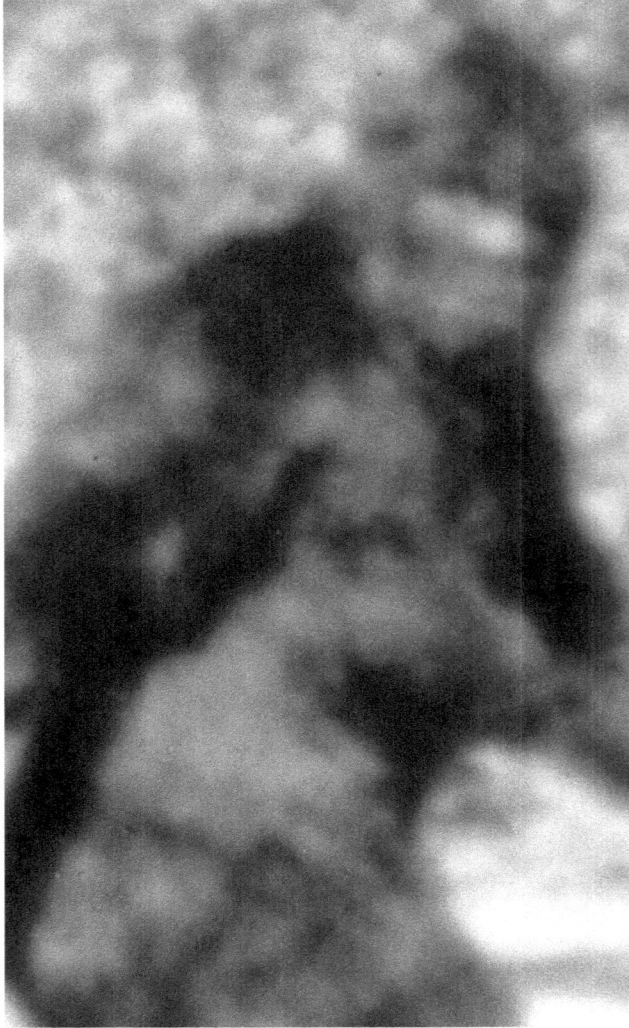

Fig. 2

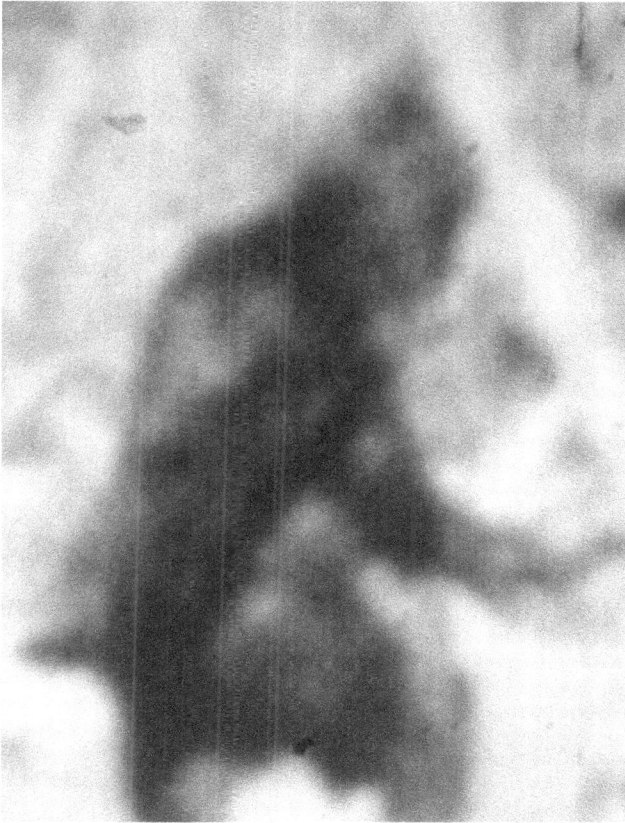

Fig. 3

Figures 1, 2, and 3 show the back of the neck before, during, and after the head turn. Bill Munns explains that this would have resulted in an exposure of the neck seam *if* Patty was an actor inside a costume.

Figures 4 and 5 are a side-by-side comparison of Patty and Harry. Notice how Harry's features are anatomically incorrect for an ape, whereas Patty has many features we see in apes, such as a brow ridge, sagittal crest, and a flat face. Remember, Munns said that it was necessary to exaggerate the features on an ape headpiece in order to fit an actor's head inside. Patty's features do not display any exaggeration.

Fig. 4a

Fig. 5a

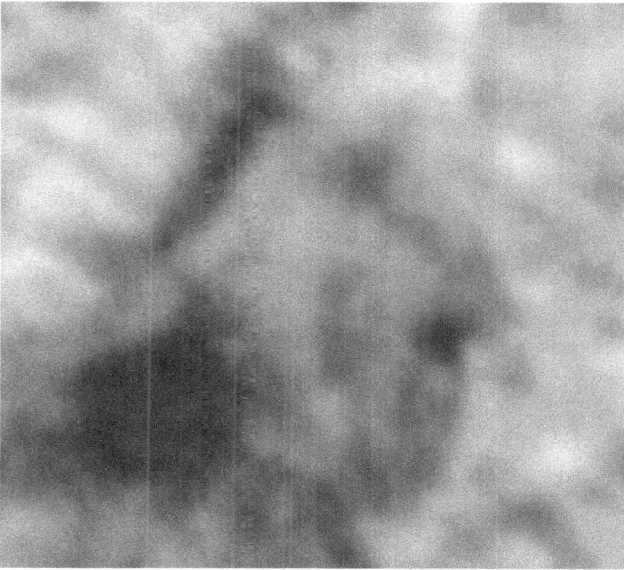

Fig 4b

Fig. 5b

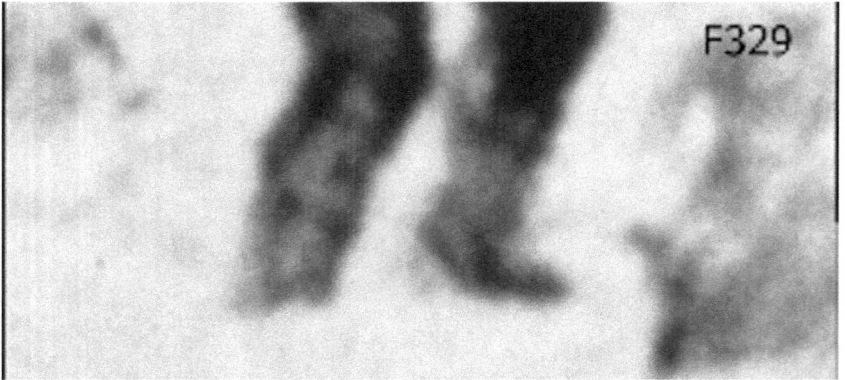

Fig. 6

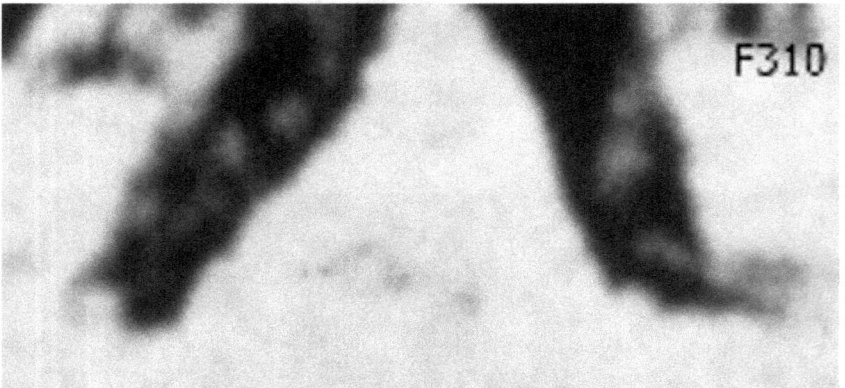

Fig. 7

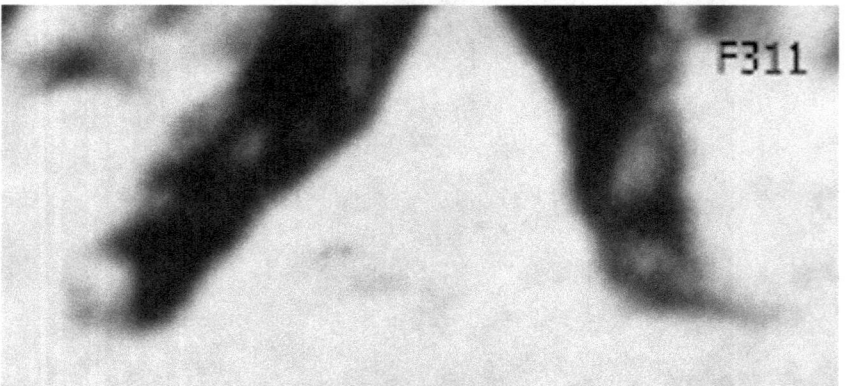

Fig. 8

Frames 329, 310, and 311 (Figures 6, 7, and 8, respectively) show Patty's feet. We can see that there is a flexibility in the foot that would have been impossible to recreate with a costume. Furthermore, this flexibility eliminates Daegling's suggestion that a foot prosthetic was used as creating such a flexible prosthetic would have been all but impossible for even the best costume designers in the world, let alone an amateur without any mechanical engineering experience.

Figure 9 shows the muscle herniation. The bulge is visible just above and to the left of the right knee. Look at the right arm, and you can also see that the triceps are flexing, another detail that would have been beyond the capability of a 1967 ape suit.

Fig. 9

Fig. 10

Fig. 11

Figures 10 and 11 are noticeably different. Daegling argues that Patterson used his drawings as a template, yet there are too many differences to assume this to be the case. The drawing in Figure 10 simply has enlarged human feet, whereas the heel in Figure 12 is extended. We can also see that Patty's breasts are noticeable, as is the muscle herniation and triceps flexion.

Fig. 12

Fig. 13

Fig. 11

Fig. 14

Fig. 4a

Figure 13 is from 1967's *King Kong Escapes*, and Figure 14 is from 1962's *King Kong vs. Godzilla*. We can see with the 1962 suit that the suit folds with the actor's movements. We do not see that in Patty. As for the suit in *King Kong Escapes*, the head structure is completely different, as is the overall shape of the body.

Figures 15 and 16 show the Myakka ape. The ape stands taller in Figure 16, but, as you can see, the ape is still not fully upright. The ape's size makes it impossible for it to be an orangutan.

Fig. 15

Fig. 16

ACKNOWLEDGMENTS

There are many people I would like to thank for their contributions to this book.

Thank you to all of the people who have researched this subject. Including but not limited to Dr. Jeff Meldrum, Dr. Grover Krantz, Dr. John Bindernagel, Bill Munns, John Green, Loren Coleman, Cliff Barackman, and James 'Bobo' Fay.

Thank you to the team at the Forest Fleur. We have spent many hours discussing Sasquatch. A big thank you to Emily Fleur for letting me come on the podcast. Your support throughout the work of this book has been amazing.

Thank you to Edward Cornthwaite once again for editing this book. Your work is nothing short of phenomenal.

Thank you to Neil TS Flanders. Your work on the cover design blew me away.

Thank you to Hangari Publishing for taking a chance on my manuscript.

Most importantly, thank you to everyone who read bought this book. Without you, I am nothing.

WORK CITED

Ang, Tom. *Fundamentals of Photography: The Essential Handbook for Both Digital and Film Cameras*. New York: Alfred A. Knopf, 2008.

Barackman, Cliff and James 'Bobo' Fay. Interview with Gareth Patterson. "Ep. 060 - South African Mystery Hominoids." *Bigfoot and Beyond with Cliff and Bobo*. Podcast Audio. June 29th, 2020. https://www.bigfootandbeyondpodcast.com/listen.

Bindernagel, John A. *North America's Great Ape: The Sasquatch: A Wildlife Biologist Looks at the Continent's Most Misunderstood Large Mammal*. Courtenay:Beachcomber Books, 1998.

Bindernagel, John. *The Discovery of the Sasquatch*. Courtenay: Beachcomber Books, 2010.

Brusatte, Steve. *The Rise and Fall of the Dinosaurs: A New History of Their World*. New York: William Morrow, 2018.

Buckley, Thomas. "Monsters and the Quest for Balance in Native Northwest California," in *Manlike Monsters on Trial: Early Records and*

Modern Evidence, eds. Marjorie Halpin and Michael M. Ames, (Vancouver: The University of British Columbia Press, 1980), 229–34.

Bynum, William. *A Little History of Science*. New Haven: Yale University Press, 2013.

Carnegie, Dale. *How to Win Friends and Influence People*. New York: Pocket Books, 1998.

Carnegie, Dale. *The Quick and Easy Way to Effective Speaking: Modern Techniques for Dynamic Communication*. New Delhi: General Press, 2018.

Carpenter, Kenneth J. "Prematurity and Delay in the Prevention of Scurvy," in *Prematurity in Scientific Discovery: On Resistance and Neglect* ed. Ernest B. Hook, (Berkely and Los Angeles: University of California Press, 2002), 87–91.

Colarusso, John. "Ethnographic Information on a Wild Man of the Caucasus," in *Manlike Monsters on Trial: Early Records and Modern Evidence*, eds. Marjorie Halpin and Michael M. Ames, (Vancouver: The University of British Columbia Press, 1980), 255–64.

Daegling, David J. *Bigfoot Exposed: An Anthropologist Examines America's Enduring Legend*. Walnut Creek: AltaMira Press, 2004.

Dewitt, Richard. *Worldviews: An Introduction to the History and Philosophy of Science*. Malden: Blackwell Publishing Ltd, 2004. FCastle6969, "Janos Prohaska." January 5th, 2008, 0:41, https://www.youtube.com/watch?v =Hd x6toQWc5g.

Fleur, Emily. Interview with Jeff Meldrum. *The Forest Fleur Bigfoot Research*. Podcast Audio. May 11th, 2020. https://podcasts.apple.com/us/podcast/campfire-chats-dr-jeff-meldrum-expert-on-science-sasquatch/id1441917844?i=1000474279895.

Gil, George W. "Population Clines of the North American Sasquatch as Evidenced by Track Lengths and Estimated Structures," in *Manlike Monsters on Trial: Early Records and Modern Evidence*, eds. Marjorie Halpin and Michael M. Ames, (Vancouver: The University of British Columbia Press, 1980), 265–73.

Gittell, Noah. "Let's Try that Again... The Most Difficult Scenes in Cinema History." *The Guardian*, March 8, 2017. https://www.the-guardian.com/film/filmblog   /2017/mar/31/most-difficult-scenes-ever-filmed-cinema-history.

Green, John. "Editorial," in *The Scientist looks at the Sasquatch*, eds. Roderick Sprague and Grover S. Krantz, (Moscow: The University of Idaho Press, 1977), 27–29.

Green, John. "What is the Sasquatch?" in *Manlike Monsters on Trial: Early Records and Modern Evidence*, eds. Marjorie Halpin and Michael M. Ames, (Vancouver: The University of British Columbia Press, 1980), 237–44.

Ilana Löwy, "Fleck. Kuhn, and Stent: Loose Reflections on the Notion of Prematurity," in *Prematurity in Scientific Discovery: On Resistance and Neglect* ed. Ernest B. Hook, (Berkely and Los Angeles: University of California Press, 2002), 295–305.

Hall, Phil. *The Weirdest Movie Ever Made*: *The Patterson-Gimlin Bigfoot Film*. Albany: BearManor Media, 2018.

Halpin, Marjorie M. "Investigating the Goblin Universe," in *Manlike Monsters on Trial: Early Records and Modern Evidence*, eds. Marjorie Halpin and Michael M. Ames. (Vancouver: The University of British Columbia Press, 1980), 3–26.

Hill, Napoleon. *Outwitting the Devil: The Secrets to Freedom and Success.* Shippensburg: Sound Wisdom, 2011.

Hook, Earnest B. "A Background to Prematurity and Resistance to Discovery," in *Prematurity in Scientific Discovery: On Resistance and Neglect* ed. Ernest B. Hook, (Berkely and Los Angeles: University of California Press, 2002), 3–21.

Krantz, Grover S. *Bigfoot: Sasquatch Evidence.* 2nd ed. Blaine: Hancock House Publishers, 2008.

Krantz, Grover S. "Introduction and Commentary," in *The Scientist looks at the Sasquatch*, eds. Roderick Sprague and Grover S. Krantz, (Moscow: The University of Idaho Press, 1977), 9–26.

Meldrum, Jeff. *Sasquatch: Legend Meets Science.* New York: BooBam Ventures, Inc., 2006.

Meyer, Stephen. *Darwin's Doubt: The Explosive Origin of Animal Life and the Case for Intelligent Design.* New York: HarperCollins Publishers, 2013.

Munns, William. *When Roger Met Patty.* CreateSpace Independent Publishing Platform, 2014.

Murphy, Christopher. *The Bigfoot Film Controversy.* Blaine: Hancock House Publishers, 2005.

Napier, John. *Bigfoot: The Yeti and Sasquatch in Myth and Reality.* Boston: E. P. Dutton & Co., Inc., 1973.

Napier, J.R. and Napier, P.H. *The Natural History of the Primates.* Cambridge: The MIT Press, 1985.

Park, Sooyong. *The Great Soul of Siberia: In Search of the Elusive Siberian Tiger.* London: William Collins, 2017.

Patterson, Gareth. *The Secret Elephants: The Rediscovery of the World's Most Southerly Elephants*. Cape Town: Penguin Books, 2011.

Peterson, Jordan. *12 Rules for Life: An Antidote to Chaos*. Toronto: Random House Canada, 2018.

Rabiger, Michael and Hubris-Cherrier, Mick. *Directing: Film Techniques and Aesthetics*. 5th ed. Burlington: Focal Press, 2013.

Rigsby, Bruce. "Some Pacific Northwest Native Language Names for the Sasquatch Phenomenon," in *The Scientist looks at the Sasquatch*, eds. Roderick Sprague and Grover S. Krantz, (Moscow: The University of Idaho Press, 1977), 31–38.

Rogan, Joe. Interview with Rick Baker. "#1377 - Rick Baker." *The Joe Rogan Experience*. Podcast audio, November 11, 2019. https://open.spotify.com/episode/oqHgRRf1LXq6IhNYZh1EOB.

Ruse, Michael. "The Prematurity of Darwin's Theory of Natural Selection," in *Prematurity in Scientific Discovery: On Resistance and Neglect* ed. Ernest B. Hook, (Berkely and Los Angeles: University of California Press, 2002), 213–38.

Serrano, Shea. "Fact-Checking Morpheus's 'Red Pill or Blue Pill' Monologue From *The Matrix*." The Ringer, January 8, 2018, accessed June 29, 2021. https://www.theringer. com/movies/2018/1/8/16861248/morpheus-neo-the-matrix-red-pill-or-blue-pill-monologue.

Sprague, Roderick. "Carved Heads of the Columbia River and Sasquatch," in *Manlike Monsters on Trial: Early Records and Modern Evidence*, eds. Marjorie Halpin and Michael M. Ames, (Vancouver: The University of British Columbia Press, 1980), 229–34.

Stent, Gunther S. "Prematurity in Scientific Discovery," in *Prematurity in Scientific Discovery: On Resistance and Neglect* edited by Ernest B.

Hook, (Berkeley and Los Angeles: University of California Press, 2002), 22–33.

Suttles, Wayne. "On the Track of the Sasquatch," in *The Scientist looks at the Sasquatch*, eds. Roderick Sprague and Grover S. Krantz, (Moscow: The University of Idaho Press, 1977), 39–76.

Suttles, Wayne. "Sasquatch: The Testimony of Tradition," in *Manlike Monsters on Trial: Early Records and Modern Evidence*, eds. Marjorie Halpin and Michael M. Ames, (Vancouver: The University of British Columbia Press, 1980), 245–54.

Taylor, Al, and Roy, Susan. *Making a Monster: The Creation of Screen Characters by the Great Makeup Artist*s. New York: Crown Publishers, 1988.

Time-Life Books. *Mysterious Creatures (Mysteries of the Unknown)*. Richmond: Time Life Education, 1988.

Townes, Charles H. "Resistance to Change and New Ideas in Physics: A Personal Perspective," in *Prematurity in Scientific Discovery: On Resistance and Neglect* ed. Ernest B. Hook, (Berkeley and Los Angeles: University of California Press, 2002), 46–58.

Tyson, Neil deGrasse. *Letters From an Astrophysicist*. New York: W. W. Norton & Company, 2019.

Walker, Matthew. *Why We Sleep: Unlocking the Power of Sleep and Dreams*. New York: Scribner, 2017.

Westrum, Ron. "Sasquatch and Scientists: Reporting Scientific Anomalies," in *Manlike Monsters on Trial: Early Records and Modern Evidence*, eds. Marjorie Halpin and Michael M. Ames, (Vancouver: The University of British Columbia Press, 1980), 27–36.

IMAGES CITATION

Figure 1—Munns, Bill. 'Images from the Patterson-Gimlin Film'. Email, 2019.

Figure 2—Munns, Bill. 'Images from the Patterson-Gimlin Film'. Email, 2019.

Figure 3—Munns, Bill. 'Images from the Patterson-Gimlin Film'. Email, 2019.

Figure 4—Munns, Bill. 'Images from the Patterson-Gimlin Film'. Email, 2019.

Figure 5—Goodloe, David. "Bigfoot in the House." Birth of a Notion, June 5th, 2017, accessed March 21, 2020. https://birth-of-a-notion.blogspot. com/2017/06/bigfoot-in-house.html.

Figure 6—Munns, Bill. The Munns Report. 2009, accessed February 4, 2020. http://themunnsreport.com/.

Figure 7—Munns, Bill. The Munns Report. 2009, accessed February 4, 2020. http://themunnsreport.com/.

Figure 8—Munns, Bill. The Munns Report. 2009, accessed February 4, 2020. http://themunnsreport.com/.

Figure 9—Munns, Bill. 'Permission for my Book'. Email, 2020.

Figure 10—Munns, Bill. 'Images from the Patterson-Gimlin Film'. Email, 2019.

Figure 11—Bigfoot Field Research Organization. "2020 Bigfoot Expeditions Open to Non-members," 2019, accessed March 21, 2020. bfro.net/ news/roundup/expeds_2020.asp.

Figure 12—Murphy, Christopher. The Bigfoot Film Controversy. Blaine: Hancock House Publishers, 2005, 121.

Figure 13—Gojipedia. "King Kong Escapes—Gallery," accessed June 29, 2021. https://godzilla.fandom .com/wiki/King_Kong_Escapes_(1967_film)/Gallery.

Figure 14—Bush, Nicholas J. "Godzilla vs. Kong Slated for 2020 Release." The Tokusatsu Network. October 14, 2015, accessed June 29, 2021. https://tokusatsunetwork.com/2015/10/godzilla-vs-king-kong-slated-for-2020-release/.

Figure 15—Coleman, Loren. "The Myakka 'Skunk Ape' Photographs," 2001–2002, accessed March 21, 2020. http://www. lorencoleman.com/myakka.html.

Figure 16—Coleman, Loren. "The Myakka 'Skunk Ape' Photographs," 2001–2002, accessed March 21, 2020. http://www. lorencoleman.com/myakka.html.

INDEX

NOTES

Introduction

1. Napoleon Hill, *Outwitting the Devil: The Secrets to Freedom and Success,* (Shippensburg: Sound Wisdom, 2011), 133.
2. Shea Serrano, "Fact-Checking Morpheus's 'Red Pill or Blue Pill' Monologue From *The Matrix*," The Ringer, January 8, 2018, accessed June 29, 2021. https://www.theringer.com/movies/2018/1/8/16861248/morpheus-neo-the-matrix-red-pill-or-blue-pill-monologue.

1. The Patterson-Gimlin Film

1. Phil Hall, *The Weirdest Movie Ever Made: The Patterson-Gimlin Bigfoot Film,* (Albany: BearManor Media, 2018), 17.
2. William Munns, *When Roger Met Patty,* (CreateSpace Independent Publishing Platform, 2014), 113.
3. Ibid., 29.
4. Christopher Murphy, *The Bigfoot Film Controversy,* (Blaine: Hancock Publishers, 2005), 185.
5. Munns, *Patty,* 29.
6. David J. Daegling, *Bigfoot Exposed: An Anthropologist Examines America's Enduring Legend,* (Walnut Creek: AltaMira Press, 2004), 109.
7. Murphy, *Controversy,* 144.
8. Joe Rogan, interview with Rick Baker, *The Joe Rogan Experience,* podcast audio, November 6 2019. https://open.spotify.com/episode/0qHgRRfiLXq6IhNYZhiEOB.
9. Ibid.
10. Ibid.
11. Al Taylor and Susan Roy, *Making a Monster: The Creation of Screen Characters by the Great Makeup Artists,* (New York: Crown Publishers, 1988), 211–12.
12. Fcastle6969, "Janos Prohaska." YouTube video, January 5, 2008, Interview, 0.40.
13. Taylor and Roy, *Making a Monster,* 258.
14. Munns, *Patty,* 182.
15. Ibid., 197.
16. Ibid.
17. Ibid., 244.
18. Noah Gittell, "Let's Try That Again... The Most Difficult Scenes to Film in Cinema History," *The Guardian,* March 31, 2017, accessed October 1, 2019.

https://www.theguardian.com/film/filmblog/2017/mar/31/most-difficult-scenes-ever-filmed-cinema-history.

19. Munns, *Patty*, 215–16.

20. Hall, *The Weirdest Movie*, 17.

21. Jordan Peterson, *12 Rules for Life: An Antidote to Chaos,* (Toronto: Random House Canada, 2018), 256.

22. Grover Krantz, *Bigfoot: Sasquatch Evidence,* 2nd ed. (Blaine: Hancock House Publishers, 2008), 116.

23. Ibid.

24. Christopher Murphy, *The Bigfoot Film Controversy*, (Blaine: Hancock Publishers, 2005), 240.

25. FCastle6969, "Janos Prohaska," January 5th, 2008, YouTube video, 0:41, https://www.youtube.com/watch ?v=Hdx 6toQWc5g.

26. Dale Carnegie, *The Quick and Easy Way to Effective Speaking: Modern Techniques for Dynamic Communication*, (New Delhi: General Press, 2018), 69.

27. Daegling, *Exposed*, 146.

28. Jeff Meldrum, *Sasquatch: Legend Meets Science*, (New York: BooBam Ventures, Inc., 2006), 175–76.

29. Munns, *Patty*, 194.

30. Ibid., 402.

31. Michael Rabiger and Mick Hubris-Cherrier, *Directing: Film Techniques and Aesthetics*, 5th ed. (Burlington: Focal Press, 2013), 167.

32. Ibid., 171.

33. Ibid., 109.

34. Munns, *Patty*, 147.

35. Time-Life Books, *Mysterious Creatures (Mysteries of the Unknown)*, (Richmond, VA: Time Life Education, 1988), 124.

36. Daegling, *Exposed*, 118.

37. Ibid., 147.

38. Ibid., 144.

39. Ibid.

40. Ibid.

41. Ibid., 146.

42. Ibid.

43. Ibid., 113.

44. Taylor and Roy, *Making a Monster*, 211–12.

45. Daegling, *Exposed*, 114.

46. Ibid.,113.

47. Tom Ang, *Fundamentals of Photography: The Essential Handbook for Both Digital and Film Cameras,* (New York: Alfred A. Knopf, 2008), 16.

48. Munns, Patty, 367–68.

49. Ibid., 368.

50. Ibid., 38.

2. The Myakka Ape Photos

1. J.R. Napier and P.R. Napier, *The Natural History of the Primates* (Cambridge: The MIT Press, 1985), 50.

3. Footprints

1. Sooyong Park, *The Great Soul of Siberia: In Search of the Elusive Siberian Tiger*, (London: William Collins, 2017). XIII.
2. Ibid., 14.
3. Ibid., 16.
4. Ibid., 19.
5. Gareth Patterson, *The Secret Elephants: The Rediscovery of the World's Most Southerly Elephants*, (Cape Town: Penguin Books, 2011), 43.
6. Ibid., 37.
7. Ibid., 19.
8. Ibid., 52.
9. Ibid., 53.
10. Ibid., 54
11. Ibid., 299.
12. Steve Brusatte, *The Rise and Fall of the Dinosaurs: A New History of Their World*, (New York: William Morrow, 2018), 24.
13. Ibid., 25.
14. Krantz, *Bigfoot,* 53.
15. John Napier, *Bigfoot, The Yeti and Sasquatch in Myth and Reality*, (New York: E. P. Dutton & Co., Inc., 1973), 124.
16. Ibid., 54.
17. Krantz, *Bigfoot,* 53.
18. Meldrum, *Legend*, 228.
19. Krantz, *Bigfoot,* 70–71.
20. Ibid., 70.
21. Jeff McRoberts, "Sasquatch Legend Meets Science." YouTube video, September 19, 2016. Documentary, 43:48. https://www.youtube.com/watch?v=2EJLVdQSiuo.
22. Meldrum, *Legend*, 256.
23. Ibid., 252.
24. Ibid.
25. Ibid.
26. Ibid.
27. George W. Gil, "Population Clines of the North American Sasquatch as Evidenced by Track Lengths and Estimated Structures," in *Manlike Monsters on Trial: Early Records and Modern Evidence*, eds. Marjorie Halpin and Michael M. Ames (Vancouver: The University of British Columbia Press, 1980), 269.
28. Meldrum, *Legend*, 94.
29. Napier, *Bigfoot*, 204.

30. Ibid.
31. Gil, "Population," 265–66.
32. Meldrum, *Legend*, 12.
33. Napier, *Bigfoot*, 215.
34. Meldrum, *Legend*, 224.
35. Ibid., 223.
36. Ibid., 234–35.
37. Ibid., 235.
38. Krantz, *Bigfoot*, 53.

4. Native American History

1. Roderick Sprague, "Carved Heads of the Columbia River and Sasquatch," in *Manlike Monsters on Trial: Early Records and Modern Evidence*, eds. Marjorie Halpin and Michael M. Ames (Vancouver: The University of British Columbia Press, 1980), 229.
2. Ibid., 233.
3. Krantz, *Bigfoot*, 143.
4. Ibid.
5. John Bindernagel, *The Discovery of the Sasquatch*, (Courtenay, British Columbia: Beachcomber Books, 2010), 169.
6. Ibid.
7. Ibid., 168.
8. Marjorie M. Halpin, "Investigating the Goblin Universe," in *Manlike Monsters on Trial: Early Records and Modern Evidence*, eds. Marjorie Halpin and Michael M. Ames (Vancouver: The University of British Columbia Press, 1980), 18–19.
9. Wayne Suttles, "On the Track of the Sasquatch," in *The Scientist looks at the Sasquatch*, eds. Roderick Sprague and Grover S. Krantz (Moscow: The University of Idaho Press, 1977), 66.
10. Ibid., 65.
11. Ibid.
12. Krantz, *Bigfoot*, 142.
13. Bruce Rigsby, "Some Pacific Northwest Native Language Names for the Sasquatch Phenomenon," in *The Scientist looks at the Sasquatch*, eds. Roderick Sprague and Grover S. Krantz (Moscow: The University of Idaho Press, 1977), 33.
14. Halpin, "Goblin," 22–23.
15. Ibid., 24.
16. John Green, "What is the Sasquatch?" in *Manlike Monsters on Trial: Early Records and Modern Evidence*, eds. Marjorie Halpin and Michael M. Ames (Vancouver: The University of British Columbia Press, 1980), 249.
17. John Colarusso, "Ethnographic Information on a Wild Man of the Caucasus," in *Manlike Monsters on Trial: Early Records and Modern Evidence*, eds. Marjorie Halpin and Michael M. Ames (Vancouver: The University of British Columbia Press, 1980), 258.
18. Krantz, *Bigfoot*, 141.

19. Meldrum, *Legend*, 75.
20. Ibid.
21. Ibid., 50.

5. History of Scientific Resistance

1. Steve Shapin, *The Scientific Revolution*, (Chicago: University of Chicago Press, 1996), 20–21.
2. William Bynum, *A Little History of Science*, (New Haven: Yale University Press, 2013), 152.
3. Richard Dewitt, *Worldviews: An Introduction to the History and Philosophy of Science*, (Malden: Blackwell Publishing Ltd, 2004), 37.
4. Dewitt, *Worldviews*, 11.
5. Bindernagel, *Discovery*, 120.
6. Brusatte, *Dinosaurs*, 326.
7. Bindernagel, *Discovery*, 3.
8. Ibid., 128.
9. Ron Westrum, "Sasquatch and Scientists: Reporting Scientific Anomalies," in *Manlike Monsters on Trial: Early Records and Modern Evidence*, eds. Marjorie Halpin and Michael M. Ames (Vancouver: The University of British Columbia Press, 1980), 34.
10. Ibid., 31.
11. Earnest B. Hook, "A Background to Prematurity and Resistance to Discovery," in *Prematurity in Scientific Discovery: On Resistance and Neglect* ed. Ernest B. Hook, (Berkeley and Los Angeles: University of California Press, 2002), 3.
12. Ibid., 6.
13. Gunther S. Stent, "Prematurity in Scientific Discovery," in *Prematurity in Scientific Discovery: On Resistance and Neglect* ed. Ernest B. Hook, (Berkeley and Los Angeles: University of California Press, 2002), 30.
14. Bindernagel, *Discovery*, 139.
15. Ibid., 224.
16. Kenneth J. Carpenter, "Prematurity and Delay in the Prevention of Scurvy," in *Prematurity in Scientific Discovery: On Resistance and Neglect* ed. Ernest B. Hook, (Berkeley and Los Angeles: University of California Press, 2002), 89.
17. Bindernagel, *Discovery*, 127.

6. The Sasquatch Paradox

1. Ibid., xi.
2. Ibid., 139.
3. Ibid., 219.
4. Daegling, *Exposed*, 107.
5. Ibid., 132.
6. Bindernagel, *Discovery*, 219.

7. Daegling, *Exposed*, 108.
8. Tyson, Neil deGrasse. Twitter Post. May 14, 2021, 8:55 AM. https://twitter.com/neiltyson/status/13932032737049 06753.
9. Neil deGrasse Tyson, *Letters From an Astrophysicist*, (New York: W. W. Norton & Company, 2019), 46.
10. Carnegie, *Public Speaking*, 69.
11. Bindernagel, *Discovery*, 209.
12. Tyson, *Letters*, 47.
13. Brusatte, *Dinosaurs*, 59.
14. Bindernagel, *Discovery*, 88.
15. Tyson, Neil deGrasse. Twitter Post. April 11, 2021, 5:47 AM.
16. Daegling, *Exposed*, 108.
17. Emily Fleur, interview with Jeff Meldrum, *The Forest Fleur Bigfoot Research,* podcast audio, May 11th, 2020. https://podcasts.apple.com/us/podcast/campfire-chats-dr-jeff-meldrum-expert-on-sciencesasquatch/id1441917844   ? i=1000474279895.
18. Daegling, *Exposed*, 108.
19. Bindernagel, *Discovery*, xi.
20. Ibid., 216.
21. Ibid., 197.
22. Krantz, *Sasquatch*, 241–42.
23. Ibid., 242.
24. Ibid.
25. Halpin, "Goblin," 3–4.
26. Bindernagel, *Discovery*, 219.
27. Dale Carnegie, *How to Win Friends and Influence People*, (New York: Pocket Books, 1998), 18.
28. Krantz, *Sasquatch*, 245.
29. Bindernagel, *Discovery*, 11.
30. Ibid., 217.
31. Stephen Meyer, *Darwin's Doubt: The Explosive Origin of Animal Life and the Case for Intelligent Design*, (New York: HarperCollins Publishers, 2013), 385.
32. Charles H. Townes, "Resistance to Change and New Ideas in Physics: A Personal Perspective," in *Prematurity in Scientific Discovery: On Resistance and Neglect* ed. Ernest B. Hook, (Berkeley and Los Angeles: University of California Press, 2002), 47.
33. Bindernagel, *Discovery*, 226.
34. John A. Bindernagel, *North America's Great Ape: The Sasquatch: A Wildlife Biologist Looks at the Continent's Most Misunderstood Large Mammal*, (Courtenay: Beachcomber Books, 1998) 148.
35. Ibid.
36. Ibid., 149.
37. Peterson, *12 Rules*, 223.
38. John Green, "Editorial," in *The Scientist looks at the Sasquatch*, eds. Roderick Sprague and Grover S. Krantz (Moscow: The University of Idaho Press, 1977), 27.
39. Halpin, "Goblin," 7.

40. Meyer, *Darwin's Doubt*, 383.
41. Michael Ruse, "The Prematurity of Darwin's Theory of Natural Selection," in *Prematurity in Scientific Discovery: On Resistance and Neglect* ed. Ernest B. Hook, (Berkely and Los Angeles: University of California Press, 2002), 234.
42. Ibid.
43. Ibid., 216.
44. Bindernagel, *Discovery*, 198.
45. Ibid.
46. Ilana Löwy, "Fleck. Kuhn, and Stent: Loose Reflections on the Notion of Prematurity," in *Prematurity in Scientific Discovery: On Resistance and Neglect* ed. Ernest B. Hook, (Berkeley and Los Angeles: University of California Press, 2002), 298.
47. Ruse, "Darwin's Theory," 215.
48. Ibid., 234.
49. Meldrum, *Legend*, 258–59.

7. Assumptions

1. Gil, "Population," 272.
2. Bindernagel, *Discovery*, 115.
3. Ibid., 121.
4. Ibid., 9.
5. Ibid.
6. Ibid., 122.
7. Ibid., 116.
8. Cliff Barackman and James 'Bobo' Fay, interview with Gareth Patterson, *Bigfoot and Beyond with Cliff and Bobo*, podcast audio, June 29th, 2020. https://www.bigfootandbeyondpodcast.com/listen.
9. Matthew, Walker, *Why We Sleep: Unlocking the Power of Sleep and Dreams*, (New York: Scribner, 2017), 72–74.
10. Ibid.
11. Ibid., 219.
12. Brusatte, *Dinosaurs*, 142–43.
13. Park, *Siberian Tiger*, 105–06.
14. Ibid.
15. Brusatte, *Dinosaurs*, 53.
16. Gil, "Population," 271.
17. Ibid.
18. Napier, *Bigfoot*, 123.
19. Krantz, "Introduction," 15.
20. Ibid.

8. The Cure

1. Brusatte, *Dinosaurs*, 39–40.
2. Ibid., 40.
3. Patterson, *Secret Elephants*, 43.
4. Ibid.
5. Ibid., 244.
6. Bindernagel, *Discovery*, 204.

Afterword

1. Ibid., 223.

www.ingramcontent.com/pod-product-compliance
Lightning Source LLC
Chambersburg PA
CBHW070111030426
42335CB00016B/2102